TRUST YOUR CAPE

*How Women Find Their Power
in Giving Back*

REBECCA POWERS

The stories in this book reflect the author's recollection of events. Details and dialogue have been re-created from memory.

Printed in the United States of America.

First printing, 2021.

Publisher:
Rebecca Powers
11107 Callanish Park Drive
Austin, TX 78750

ISBN-13:978-0-578-82624-0

DEDICATION

This book is dedicated to my brother Peter
and his two rock star kids,
Ryan and Corie.

FOREWORD

I met Rebecca Powers when she invited me to be the keynote speaker at Impact Austin's first Speaker Series event in 2008. I was intrigued by the organization's collective giving model and wanted to engage with these women, many of whom were new to philanthropy. As an author and seasoned philanthropist myself, I relish the opportunity to challenge women to reach their full giving potential. That one evening in Austin, TX, confirmed for me that Rebecca had created a winning formula when she founded Impact Austin. Her warmth and effervescent personality won me over from the start. She understands the power of connecting like-minded women and introduced me to two members she knew would be interested in my philanthropic passions. Those relationships continue to this day.

Impact Austin has shepherded over 2000 women on their philanthropic journeys since 2003. Being new to philanthropy herself at the time, Rebecca had no idea that her organization would establish itself as a leader in its field. Her ability to get women excited about giving back comes from the fact that she didn't start this journey until she was 48, and there is no time to lose! This book chronicles her journey with a realness that makes you want to know more. She didn't do it alone, and the women who joined her are a big part of the story. The lessons she learned about leadership, role modeling, authentic relationships and letting go can be attributed to those talented women who helped build and sustain the organization.

The journey did not end when Rebecca retired from Impact Austin in 2011. She continues to share her experience and lessons learned with women across the country who are starting their own collectives, and her joy in paying her success forward is another reason you won't put this book down until you've read the last word. What I like about this book is the genuineness with which Rebecca tells her story. She is remarkably candid. You will feel her pain and her joy as she "trusts her cape" and encourages you to do the same.

Lynne Twist, Author
The Soul of Money

PRAISE FOR
TRUST YOUR CAPE

"Armed with passion and grit, Rebecca started a movement in Austin, TX, that has given ordinary women a philanthropic voice they didn't know they previously had. Throughout *Trust Your Cape,* you will witness her resolve to establish Impact Austin as a change agent—helping ordinary women discover their philanthropic passions, which results in their pocketbooks opening wider as they realize their full giving potential. Rebecca's ability to laugh at herself when she messes up and her willingness to learn from her mistakes make her believable and someone you want to get to know better."

—Caroline Adams Miller, MAPP,
best-selling author of *Getting Grit,* Speaker and Educator

"How often do you get to go behind the scenes and travel with a group of people that had one goal: to make an "extraordinary" impact on the people in their community? Many books will simply tell you what happened, but Rebecca puts you right there so you can see and feel it. The highs and lows. The confidence and doubts. The decisions they made and the work they put in. She offers undeniable lessons on leadership, building the right team, and what can happen when passion teams up with people who possess the intelligence, the drive, and a very powerful purpose."

—Kevin Eastman,
Amazon best-selling author of *Why the Best Are the Best*,
NBA World Championship Coach - Boston Celtics, Speaker

"Rebecca taps into something brilliant in *Trust Your Cape*: the world-changing momentum that a group of women can have when united by a common purpose. If you need to awaken to the power you have to harness your purpose through giving and concentrated generosity, then this is a must read. Her energy and joy are contagious, and her authenticity brings her story to life. You will find yourself in these pages."

—Jessica Honegger,
founder and Co-CEO, Noonday Collection,
author of *Imperfect Courage*

"Rebecca draws you in with her powerful stories about building Impact Austin and the lessons she learned as a leader. Her authenticity and sense of humor make this book easy to read, and you will want to be her friend by the time you finish. Rebecca pays her success forward by mentoring women in other cities as they create their own collective giving organizations, and there is no doubt in my mind it will be her legacy. She is the ultimate Rippler in my opinion! *Trust Your Cape's* message is timeless, actionable and it will motivate you to want to give back. So find your cape and get ready to be inspired!"

—Steve Harper,
entrepreneur & author of *The Ripple Effect:*
Maximizing the Power of Relationships for Your Life and Business

"My favorite books are always the ones written by women who share their life challenges in an honest, thoughtful way. Rebecca Powers has done just this. Not only has she used remarkable skill and perseverance to create a women's collective giving organization, Impact Austin, that has funneled more than $7 million into the community and inspired countless women's groups across the country to do the same, but she has given us tools so we, too, can make a difference. After reading *Trust Your Cape*, I feel I just need to put on my cape and fly!"

—Julie Fritz,
Impact 100, Richmond, Virginia

"Rebecca Powers turned personal trauma into a healing tool— not only for herself but for an entire community. Best of all, she teaches us how we can all make a difference in this inspiring and very human story. *Trust Your Cape* moved me to want to be a better person."

—Kevin Salwen,
author of *The Power of Half* and
some other random stuff

ACKNOWLEDGEMENTS

This book is covered in more love than I deserve, and there are so many who inspired its telling and contributed to its success.

First, the women associated with Impact Austin, who made this story possible:

- Colleen Willoughby, the pioneer of the collective giving movement and initial author of the model Impact Austin follows. There would be no Impact Austin and no *Trust Your Cape* story without her. She mentored me early on and still inspires me with her wisdom since the day we met in 2007.

- Wendy Steele, founder of Impact 100 in Cincinnati, OH, who caught my attention via the *People* magazine article at a time when I needed something positive to focus on.

- The Kitchen Table Six—Cindy, Glenda, Jane, Nancy and Phylis, who joined me as we made magic happen because we believed in our mission and each other. Our mutual respect continues to this day, and the fun we had building Impact Austin will never be duplicated.

- Our 126 founding members who believed in us before we delivered on our promise. I applaud and appreciate each of you.

- Sally, who nominated me for the 2006 KVUE *Five Who Care Community Service Award* and KVUE for giving me the award, which acknowledged that Impact Austin met an important need in our community: helping women find their power in giving back.

- Women who invested in Impact Austin during my tenure and beyond, giving their best to make Impact Austin its best:

  - Dawn, who took the hand-off from Phylis and tirelessly rocked membership recruiting early on, and Becky, who took the hand-off from Dawn, eventually getting us to 500 members and keeping us there under her watch.

  - Anna, Betsy, Connie and Becky, who led the grantmaking process and achieved stellar results.

  - Lisa and Dina, who built Girls Giving Grants from the ground up. Dina, especially, who gave nine years to the effort and raised some incredible young leaders in the process.

  - Meeta, a true team player, who didn't leave when the chips were down and propped me up when I needed it most.

  - Kathrine, who did a lot of heavy lifting behind the scenes and always made me look good. And, I mean always.

  - Sara, who inspired the establishment of the endowment and made the first investment in it.

  - Board members, too many to name, who brought special gifts and talents to bear during times of uncertainty and change. Sheroes in my book. All of them.

- Lauren, who led our board at a pivotal time and challenged everyone to dream bigger...until we did! And then, Susan, who lent her expertise as our next board leader and embraced those dreams, which made Impact Austin even better.

- Christina, who arrived with energy and passion that changed our trajectory in the BEST way.

- Judi, Linda and Phaedra on the Marketing Committee who publicized this book on social media and other mediums to help get the word out.

Thanks to each of you for holding Impact Austin in the palms of your hands and caring so deeply about its success. It made the story that much more fun to write.

Korey Howell, who took the photo that graces the cover of this book. Her work is sheer perfection..

Alicia Dunams and Toccara Ross with "Bestseller in a Weekend", who encouraged me to tell my story and coached me through the writing and publishing process. They didn't care that I had a partial draft sitting in a drawer for ten years gathering dust— they knew just what I needed to do to make the book a reality.

Susan Nunn, my editor, who challenged me to dig deeper. All because she believed in me and my story and wanted me to be proud of every word. In the process, I began to believe in myself. She helped me tell this story with my heart leading the way.

Bernadette Noll, who made personalized bookmarks, and Tracy Nelson who designed clay replicas of a woman in a cape for me to share with special supporters.

Wendy, Julie and Amy, who read my early manuscript, gave feedback and walked beside me in the writing process. Listening to my insecurities and holding space for me to question my ability when I was running out of words.

Barton Bryan (Mindset Forge), Steve Harper (Ripple Effect) and Alicia Dunams (Authoring Life), who enthusiastically invited me to share my story on their podcasts.

Lorene, who turned a fun idea into reality by designing and sewing a yellow cape for me to wear when signing books and speaking publicly.

Brett, my brother from another mother, who lost his sister to cancer…just like I lost Peter. Our bond is pretty freakin' strong. And, I don't take it for granted.

Women in other cities who have started collectives of their own and have invited me to share my experience in building Impact Austin as a way to inspire their journeys.

Allison, who continued to invest in Impact Austin as she was building Impact Grants Chicago. She is still a member of both, and we learn from her now!

Shelley and Laurie, who built Impact Central Illinois in my hometown of Peoria. Their belief in the model and in the giving spirit of their city produced phenomenal results. I am proud to be a member.

Lynne Twist, author of *The Soul of Money*, who wrote the foreword and taught me to move from a scarcity mindset to one of abundance. I now give back in ways I never thought I could. She taught me I can—and always could.

My sister, Amy, who helps me market this book to podcasters and speaking audiences so that I can sell more books and fuel the Impact Austin endowment. She is my Chief Cape Wrangler and partner in crime as we build the *Trust Your Cape* brand and dream about the future. Her dedication to this endeavor is humbling, and we're having more fun than should be considered legal.

My brother, Michael, and his lady, Cass, who proofread the final manuscript and continually cheered me on during the writing process.

My kids, Brad and Claire, who taught me how to be a better mother. Their mother. They continue to make me proud and are my favorite humans under forty. Claire helped behind the scenes as I wrote, supporting me with technical assistance due to my lack of knowledge and unwillingness to learn. Her patience and allegiance were unwavering. Brad pushed me along in the process by checking in on my progress and not accepting excuses I might have for being "stuck."

My husband, Phil, who never ever said "no" to me as I built and led Impact Austin—even in the tough times. Thank you for supporting me enthusiastically on this writing journey—giving me space to write without distraction and cheering for me when I emerged from my cave on occasion, having had a breakthrough. Your love, patience, generosity and sense of humor got me through this. I love you!

And finally, to every person who has contributed to the Impact Austin endowment—past, present and future. You understand the importance of assuring our permanence, and that is simply beautiful!

TABLE OF CONTENTS

'THE BEGINNING'

"No one else has your voice or your story.
Your story is worth telling."

—Shauna Niequist

My tastebuds came alive as the aroma of all the delicious foods that are Austin's trademark drifted past me as we deplaned and started down the jetway and into the concourse. I'm home. I found it strange. It was the foods that I loved—their aromas that brought me right back to the present, to home, to our love of our adopted town, Austin, Texas. After nine years, it was truly our home. But, as tempting as the foods were, I knew at this moment food wasn't what I needed.

The last few days I had been in California, sitting with my brother and the rest of our family, trying deep within myself to believe he would get better, but knowing that possibility was slim. Just talking, that nervous talk, trying to get things said, like remembering when Peter was five, walking behind the next door neighbor's gardener to pick up the cigarette butts he had recently tossed in the yard as he mowed, trying to take a puff before getting caught. It never worked out, though his determination was impressive. We each told our own versions of him teaching me to drive a stick shift in the high school parking lot in our old, off-white Volkswagen Beetle. I thought I was a quick study, and he countered with a reminder of his constant refrain, "Don't ride the clutch, Sis!" I knew he loved being my teacher, and I secretly liked being his student.

Peter could hardly contain his laughter, even though his voice was faint, as he recounted our one-week family road trips in the summer with six of us squeezed into that off-white Volkswagen Beetle. It was our first new car, so we didn't mind the cramped quarters. My younger sister sat in what we called "the engine," the thin, open compartment separating the back seat from the engine that is designed to hold a suitcase or two. By her sitting there, my brothers and I shared the back seat with little room to spare. Mom deftly packed all of our clothes in two suitcases that fit in the trunk at the front of the car, and off we went.

My mother established a fun tradition that caught passengers in cars that whizzed by us off-guard. You could see fingers pointing as they counted six of us crowded into our "Bug." Their facial expressions ran the gamut: surprise, disgust, humor, confusion, you name it. Whenever Mom said, "One, Two, Three, Family Look," our six expressionless faces turned left in unison, and we stared at the people looking back at us. We all cracked up when those gawkers immediately turned away as if they had no interest in us, which we knew was not true.

Peter laughed til his stomach hurt. We held hands in solidarity, though the look in his eyes let me know he was hurting more than he let on and confirmed for me that his days were numbered.

My heart was heavy when I stepped onto the plane to return to Austin. It was a night flight and as I stared out the window of the plane, seeing city lights below, then the deep black of nothingness, but knowing full well, there was never just nothing. I stared into that black slate of emptiness, wondering about life, why are the lives of good people cut short and what will the future hold for Peter's kids who were so devoted to him, and what lesson about dying are we all supposed to learn from this? But about the time we leveled off at thirty thousand feet, I could feel my heart opening to possibilities. I knew it must be Peter telling me to get on with my dreams.

An article in a magazine that I bought at the airport was all it took, and the idea started to unfold within me. I could feel the warmth of Peter's presence. A sense of excitement emerged as I was thinking about telling Phil when I got home of this organization I had dreamed up.

By the time I landed, I had worked out many of the wider view details in my mind. I didn't know if this whole idea would even survive the light of day, but I wanted to try. I wondered how Phil would take it because he had decided to retire in a couple of months. In addition to normal family duties, he planned to sleep in, work out, and play golf regularly—activities he missed as an executive of a high tech start-up. I encouraged him in his new priorities because he had worked tirelessly to support our family culminating in him traveling four million air miles in a ten-year span. This kept him away from home too much, and he looked forward to decompressing and getting to know his kids and wife again. Maybe this idea was just my own mind finding something to occupy my thoughts, or maybe Peter took that moment of quiet in midair to inspire me into moving forward.

Here at the Austin airport, fabulous aromas of barbeque and Mexican foods enveloped my path, reminding me this was one of the reasons why we fell in love with Austin years ago. Live music, fabulous foods, millionaires in ragged blue jeans, good schools, entrepreneurs, and a town that stayed young and vibrant.

Austin, Texas sure knows how to welcome people with food as soon as their feet hit the ground. I thought what an awesome way to greet strangers, just like bringing them into your own kitchen. Food being the universal language, may be one of the reasons why young entrepreneurs with grand ideas and even bigger dreams who want to change the world flock to this city. If it's not the "Keep Austin Weird" vibe that permeates our town, it might be all of the eateries that started here, many of which can be found at the airport.

I got to the car, settled in and headed home, which is about a forty minute drive. It was close to midnight, and the city lights lit up the sky. That skyline, I thought, has changed over the years. It's peppered with tall buildings that pop up seemingly overnight. So different from the way it was when we came.

I felt the tears start again, soft and silent. Nothing ever stays the same. It reminds me that more buildings are coming, which means more jobs and more people. A growing economy and a booming high-tech presence have their disadvantages when it comes to protecting the landscape that made Austin so attractive in the first place. Newer residents call it progress. Others, like us, aren't sure what to call it.

Entrepreneurs are commonplace and find each other easily. More importantly they partner with investors who support them as they work together to create magic. While not every great idea turns into a profitable business, there is no shame in failing forward here. In fact, it happens often. Failures are simply seen as temporary setbacks on the way to solving big problems that just need a different approach. Somehow, that keeps the positive energy flowing and people believing that anything is possible. Businesses develop in garages and old warehouses—wherever the rent is cheap or free. Living on ramen noodles and cereal makes life affordable, and pretention does not exist. The laid back vibe of the city yields a casualness that welcomes visitors and new residents alike. Our family felt it the day we moved here in early 1994, and I don't believe my husband has worn one of his many business suits since then.

I drove past a large field, sure it was dark, but I knew it was there. All of a sudden, I was wishing for a gentler time, thinking of the Bluebonnets, our state flower. This field, like so many others will be filled with these gorgeous flowers come spring. I would love to go sit in a field filled with these happy blue creatures, knowing my new ideas of a business would blossom just like the Bluebonnets in the spring, and my brother right there with me.

I remember people putting their kids in the middle of the fields just for a picture of them among these gorgeous flowers. We did, too. This has always been such a popular activity that the Department of Public Safety issues safety warnings with regard to those who pull off the road to take such pictures. Right now, in this moment, I had no problem imagining myself sitting among the bluebonnets at sunrise, the flowers swaying in the breeze. I smiled just with the thought of me sitting there, spreading my dreams, planting the seed of this new idea, letting it take root.

1

AHA MOMENT

*"Sorrow prepares you for joy. It violently sweeps everything out
of your house, so that new joy can find space to enter. It shakes
the yellow leaves from the bough of your heart, so that fresh
leaves can grow in their place."*

—Rumi

That momentous midair revelation occurred on January 20, 2003,
when an inexplicable sensation rolled through me, as if lifting
me from my narrow seat onto a thin cloud of warm air. It wasn't
obvious to anyone around me, but still the lightness had become
a part of me. Stuffing the open magazine in the seatback pocket
in front of me, my eyes darted around again to see if anyone was
noticing me. Still, the warmth and lightness continued. Ahhh! It
finally hit me. Wake up, Rebecca, that's what it was saying. Wake
up! The article in the magazine in front of me was the foretelling
of my future, and God punctuated that message by giving me a
visible sign. In a single moment, my life's direction changed, and

my sad heart knew it could rejoice again. God was going to be the wind beneath my wings. So, I started making plans....

People had always landed in my mailbox every Thursday afternoon for at least twenty-five years, and by Friday night, I had read every article. It feeds the shallow part of me, and I carry no shame! No article ever moved me to action until that memorable plane flight when I read about Impact 100 in Cincinnati and its founder, Wendy Steele. She convinced 122 women to join her in pooling their individual $1000 donations and giving all of that money in one lump sum to a dental clinic for the homeless.

Without hesitation, I knew I could do something like this in Austin and believed this "little" project would be the salve that soothed the hole left in my heart when Peter died. Central Texas had almost 1,000,000 residents. There had to be at least one hundred women in that number who could write a $1000 check, and I was determined to find them. I pushed any doubt to the back of my mind. I hadn't even had time to grieve, not knowing grief alone is so powerful that it would take my sails out to sea a few times before I healed. As I look back now, I was so naïve, but that was probably what saved me.

My mind kept moving forward, thinking, designing, I just couldn't let go. The investment amount made sense to me, and I looked forward to amplifying my and other women's voices in our community by combining these contributions. Without hesitation, I started a mental list of prospects before the plane landed. Oh, the possibilities!

For four days, Phil and I talked off and on about the idea. We found ourselves gravitating to our usual spots when discussing meaty subjects, with him in the recliner and me on the sofa at right angles to each other. After listening to my initial excitement, he asked questions that made me examine my motives and visualize what success looked like in my eyes. I respected his decision-making in business matters because I had witnessed it firsthand at IBM.

When we met, I had been at IBM for five years, and all of us on the sales team were like family. He was young, and we made life hard on him at first. But, he totally got us and knew he had to pay his dues to be respected and embraced. He did that in spades by taking our ribbing in stride as he went out and sold the pants off of all of us! His sales accomplishments as a rookie were epic. He did it without fanfare, but he knew how to work smart and help others along the way.

As Phil moved through his career at IBM and then at a successful start-up, he garnered respect because he treated everyone fairly, encouraged the less capable, and led his teams with appreciation for each team member. Colleagues—those who were his bosses and those who worked for him—sang his praises. He had high expectations, and he would do anything to help others be successful. He was as honest as the day is long, and I was very proud of him and his accomplishments.

But right now, I just wanted him to be as excited as I was about this new idea. Instead, his pragmatic approach to decision-making put a damper on my idealistic thinking.

"What is your end goal? How will you know if you are successful?"

"It's two-pronged. Finding at least one hundred women to contribute $1000 each by December 31 and then extending a $100,000 grant to a non-profit next June on Peter's birthday."

"What if you don't find one hundred women?"

Surprising myself and without hesitation, I replied, "That's not an option. I've never been more sure of something in my life. I will figure it out just like I had to figure out how to make my IBM sales quota years ago."

"It sounds like a lot of work in an arena you know nothing about. Are you going to ask others to help you, or is this a solo act?"

"Well, I've already shared my idea with my Bible study group, and two women want to invest and also help me build this thing. I know I can do it, and I'm asking you to trust me, even though I don't have all the answers right now."

"How will this affect our family, you know, me and the kids?"

"Somehow, I'll make it work. They are teenagers and don't need me as much as they used to. You are about to retire, and I'm hoping you'll be available to help out at times. I've been retired for thirteen years, and I'm ready for a new challenge—especially one that will teach me about my community and help heal the hole in my heart at the same time."

In the end, he was mildly supportive and said, "Reb, you have to try this. You'll never know what's possible if you don't go for it."

Neither one of us realized what lay ahead, and it's just as well we didn't. Some amount of naivete is healthy—a lesson I learned over and over as Impact Austin took shape. Though, this was in God's hands. The wind beneath my cape was His, and I was just the vessel. When I am obedient, He is faithful.

After the long conversation with Phil, my mind slowly drifted to thoughts of Peter and what he might think of my plan. I believed he'd be proud of me for taking a leap of faith and trying something I felt called to do. He'd no doubt cheer me on, but he would not want any of it to be about him. I knew this because over the ten weeks leading up to his passing, Peter and I shared pieces of ourselves that few knew, using Instant Messenger to communicate.

He scolded me about two of the guys I dated in high school solely because they owned cool cars, which I deny to this day, thank you very much. Dave drove a 1969 white Z28 Camaro with orange stripes, and Casey drove a deep blue 1966 Pontiac GTO with a rebuilt engine that accelerated from a stoplight like nobody's business. I truly didn't care about cars—just the boys driving them.

We reminisced about Peter's days working at the bowling alley in high school and how he loved setting pins and troubleshooting at the back of the lanes where he could smoke cigarettes in solitude. A really great night included a beer or two as they were cleaning the lanes after closing. Underage drinking and smoking were not condoned, but neither carried the stigma it does today.

We laughed more than once about the trip we took to Australia in 1973 to visit our parents, who had moved to Melbourne with our younger sister and brother for my father's job. Peter was in the Navy, and we met up at LAX to fly together. When our flight landed, and as people cleared customs, they passed through a sliding glass door where all of the locals waited to welcome their visitors from the US. When that door opened the first time, I saw our parents and siblings waving wildly. We hadn't seen them in nine months, and I was aching to walk through that door and hug them. We were so close!

As we approached the immigration official's booth, Peter looked around and saw a couple behind us that seemed exceptionally eager to reunite with their family—as if we were not! He insisted they move ahead of us in line. Really, Peter? He was kind to a fault, and this was one time when I let my irritation get the best of me—embarrassing him instead of celebrating one of his finer qualities. It reminded each of us as to how differently we approached life. At least we could finally laugh about it via the keyboard!

We also discussed death. While scared of passing, he accepted his fate, and I drew courage from that. At times, I called him on his 'bull——', which fostered more honest conversations with the tips of our fingers flying across our keyboards than we ever had in person or voice to voice. It was safe, and we said what came to us from our hearts. I even shared the promise of eternal life as I understand it…knowing it was his to accept, or not—that was between him and God. Peter never told me if he acted on the invitation, and I have no doubt he did.

Tears flowed down my face often as we typed back and forth. He must have known because he routinely came back with quick-witted responses at just the right moment to lift my spirits. Who was supposed to be comforting whom? Because we couldn't see or hear each other, I envisioned my brother from a few years earlier with his lips getting thinner the wider he smiled, with his brown eyes twinkling, and the kindness of his countenance exuding a sense of calm. While most of that was gone now, his mind never dulled, and he never lost his dry wit, even when struggling to type.

Sometimes, he'd end a conversation abruptly because he just couldn't continue. He wouldn't elaborate. He'd just say, "Love ya,

Reb. Gotta go." I'd check back occasionally to see when he was online again and pick up right where we left off. The gift Peter left me was a glimpse into his heart that had never been open to me before.

While Peter knew he was passing, he didn't focus on his plight. He chose "Angel" by Sarah McLachlan for his memorial service. Sitting in silence and tears at that service, the lyrics took on a very special meaning, reminding me of the lightness I felt in midair back in January. For Peter, the lyrics metaphorically represented a release from his earthly body and his escape from pain, and we have been deeply connected ever since. Amazingly, Sarah's song plays on the radio when discouragement and despair set in, which is a sure sign to me that Peter is perched on my left shoulder telling me, "It's gonna be okay, Reb." It's his way of encouraging me to keep going and to trust my cape.

From the moment I returned from the memorial service, I never looked back. I had already scared up some excitement with my neighbors about Impact Austin, and although I had read that grief could move in on me in waves, I tried to stay ahead of it all by bringing Peter's memory along with me. By focusing on building the organization with other women, it took my mind off of my sadness. Since Peter and I didn't see each other very often, it wasn't his physical presence I missed. I wanted to sit down at the computer and check—aching for him to be signed on so we could chat.

One time in particular, when it hit me that he was never going to sign on again, my body physically crumbled. I was sitting at my desk with my feet in my chair and my knees touching my chest, when my wailing produced tears that were streaming down my face and onto my knees as they drenched both my clothes and my skin. I knew I needed to send an apology. I began typing, "Peter, I am so sorry for any way I let you down when you were alive. I still love you so much, and I will never forsake your kids—no matter what." Sobs continued as my head bobbed up and down, accompanying the uneven breaths I had taken in as I let my emotions out.

All of a sudden my head lifted. It's as if Peter was raising my head for me and telling me it's okay and that he will never **really** leave me. Whoa. It felt spooky. My eyes continued looking straight ahead, a bit worried that a miniature Peter was sitting on my left shoulder with that same mischievous smile I used to hate. Instead, a feeling of total calm enveloped me. Putting my feet back on the floor, I sat up a little straighter and continued with my work. My heart felt a bit lighter, and I felt loved.

We have a few picture drawers at home where we have always kept photos we've taken, or been given, over the years. One day, not long after the memorial service, I pulled out those drawers and looked for any picture with him in it. My favorite has always been his official Navy picture, which was on top. Every sailor has one taken early in their service life. Peter was all of nineteen at the time and had the greatest smile. Photographs of Peter with his children came tumbling out next. The innocence of their smiles as young ones and the loving smile on Peter's face reminded me of his devotion to them. Every now and then, it's fun to look at those photos. I still grin when I see his eyes gazing back at me.

Even now, his children, Corie and Ryan, stay in steady contact and visit us occasionally. They are young adults with busy lives, but we all stay connected on some level—even if it's just knowing we have family in other parts of the country that love us. Ryan looks like Peter. He has the same twinkle in his eye that his father had, and it's not surprising that Ryan never tires of hearing that. He proudly wears a tattoo on his chest over his heart in the shape of a golf ball with the inscription "Dad" that includes his date of birth and date of death.

Corie, a skilled soccer player, still misses seeing her dad on the sidelines at her games. Peter travelled five or six hours each way to see her play on weekends—that's just how he was. We seem to tell the same Peter/Dad stories when we're together—laughing just as hard each time, knowing he is in heaven laughing with us.

2

PUTTING A STAKE IN THE GROUND

"There is no power for change greater than a community discovering what it cares about."

—Margaret J. Wheatley

Prior to Peter's passing, Phil and I took on very stereotypical roles as husband and wife, father and mother. I loved staying at home with the kids after my IBM sales career. I also took great pride in supporting Phil as he advanced in his career, which meant I was the "glue" at home that kept everything running smoothly so that when he was available on the weekends, he didn't have to do anything but hang with the kids and love on them. We reserved Friday evenings for family time, which usually meant playing Elton John, Bruce Springsteen and Meatloaf CD's while the kids jumped over the sofa (no, really) and did summersaults as Phil and I sang at the tops of our lungs. It didn't take long for the kids to learn all of the lyrics, and then we sang as a quartet. Though Brad and I maintain to this day that Claire and Phil cannot carry a tune. So we just sing louder to drown them out.

We reserved Saturday nights for going out to dinner as a couple or to social gatherings. Over good steak and fine wine, we talked about our weeks. Issues with the kids that I needed advice about. Work-related stuff for Phil. I was more inquisitive about his work than he had the patience for; so, I prioritized my questions according to what I wanted to know most. When his eyes started glazing over and he asked for the check, I knew my curiosity had tired him out, and he was out of words—any words!

We'd return home, sit on the couch, hold hands and listen to the Les Miserables soundtrack. It was our favorite dessert. We've seen the musical three times, and it always messes with our hearts. Phil connects with Eponine's storyline of redemption, and I delight in the Marius-Cosette love story which feeds my hopeless romantic tendencies.

I fretted for days before contacting *People* for the contact info of the lady who unbeknownst to her, had inspired me. That bit of fear of not being good enough or not being taken seriously caused temporary inertia. If she wouldn't talk to me, where would all of this be?

Finally, I did it. I called and got the information, and then I was second-guessing myself while I waited for her response. I had lots of thoughts about how our first interaction would play out. Will she be happy I want to copy her idea? Will she be friendly and helpful? Will she think I can pull this off? Should I act like I have a clue or admit I have no idea what I'm doing—just that I knew the idea was fabulous?

I had visited the Impact 100 website several times to understand as much as I could about their structure and how they operated. I had read the bios of their eighteen board members and felt a bit intimidated. The founder, Wendy Steele, had an impressive resume, having held leadership positions in the Junior League and Garden Club. She was a banker by profession and regularly volunteered in her community. She was well-connected and had lots of contacts. I, on the other hand, had done very little volunteering—just for my kids' PTA and Sunday school. For a fleeting moment, I questioned my ability to pull this off.

Then, it hit me—what would brand Impact Austin differently than Impact 100 was our **grassroots** approach to philanthropy. I was determined to see if "ordinary" women could make an "extraordinary" impact and convinced myself the worst thing that could happen was I'd raise $20,000 instead of $100,000. Still not shabby for someone who had never given a penny to help her community.

We had agreed to talk by phone, and a moment before our call took place, I consciously chose to stand between my kitchen table and the counter looking through the picture window that overlooked the canyon behind our house. Standing made me feel more confident and professional, and I wanted this stranger to take me seriously. By facing the window, I could take in the calmness of the canyon and hopefully feel more relaxed.

When Wendy answered the phone, her warmth grabbed me. "Hi, Rebecca, it's so nice to talk to you, and I congratulate you on your tenacity in navigating the *People* gauntlet to find me. Tell me a little bit about yourself and how I can help you."

"I am so excited about the possibility of starting an organization like yours in Austin, Texas. I know I can find one hundred women who can contribute $1000 in order to make a $100,000 grant to a non-profit in town. My brother recently passed, and working on this will feel like salve for the hole in my heart. Let's just say I have a personal motivation to make this happen. How did you arrive at this giving model?"

"The idea percolated in my head for a while before I took action. My favorite aspect of the model revolves around our voting process. By giving each member one vote by secret ballot when choosing each year's grant recipient, it gives each member equal power."

I liked that a lot and absorbed her words like a sponge, capturing all of it at my kitchen table. My handwriting became increasingly illegible as I recorded her comments. With the phone buried in the crook of my neck and with two cats trying to bite my pen as it flew across the page, I was falling in love with the possibilities.

Thank goodness technology was not as advanced as it is today because I was in my terrycloth bathrobe with no makeup on and unruly curls covering my head. Eventually, I found myself slouching and taking notes as if being in class with a revered professor whose every word mattered.

Wendy's motivation to start Impact 100 was different than mine in that she was using what she had learned from her previous philanthropic experiences to get more women involved in giving back. I was new to philanthropy and planned to use Impact Austin to teach myself and others about giving back and experiencing the power of women pooling their financial resources to effect positive change. I didn't have any previous experience upon which to build the foundation for Impact Austin—just powerful dreams that created possibilities that would turn into success as Impact Austin was sure to grow roots. In my heart I knew it was a leap of faith, but hey, I had been taking these leaps most of my life and it had been a while since the last one, so it was time.

As she and I talked, my vision for Impact Austin became clearer. My voice got louder and louder and more excited as the conversation continued.

Wendy commented, "Your passion and excitement are off the charts. If you dot your i's and cross your t's, you will have a great chance at success."

"Somehow, I believe that, too."

It also gave me the courage to ask an important question, "Are you willing to share your bylaws with us, so we don't have to reinvent the wheel?" I figured by seeing how they governed themselves, it would help us get started even faster.

She replied firmly, "We're in Cincinnati. You are in Austin. Our organization cannot add value there. You have to figure this out on your own and make decisions independently from us."

Panic rolled through me. Were my insecurities showing through? At first, I was miffed and a bit deflated—already in an environment I wasn't familiar with and getting the feeling that she wasn't all that interested in helping us be successful. But, her next sentence gave me all the encouragement I needed to keep going.

"Go to the Council on Foundations' website and order *First Steps in Starting a Foundation*. It will give you a roadmap and will help you make some critical decisions that will guide your success."

Before hanging up, I thanked her and promised, "You can count on Impact Austin to be the first Impact 100 descendant to extend a $100,000 grant as a result of reading the article in *People*."

With a smile in her voice, she replied, "I've fielded dozens of calls regarding the magazine article, and you have some stiff competition from others who are interested in doing the same thing in their locales."

That comment spurred me on even more. Still happily clueless as to how all of this would unfold, I decided to become friends with my computer and figure out how to order that seemingly all-important book.

Ordering the how-to book was the easy part, and it arrived a couple of weeks later. As I was pulling it out of the mailbox, lots of questions came to mind. Are the words going to seem like gibberish or a foreign language? How much of a learning curve will there be? Am I really up to this challenge? Peter patiently whispered in my ear, telling me not to feel discouraged and to go for it. I knew that large white envelope held the roadmap to success, and I ripped into it when I got inside the house. The book looked intimidating...that's when I called Glenda, one of our founding board members.

As Impact Austin began to take shape, I had to get busy finding women to help me build this organization—not just attend meetings, but roll up their sleeves and make stuff happen. We had to incorporate our business, establish bylaws, apply for 501(c)3 nonprofit status, define our mission, vision and values, create member recruitment packets and marketing flyers, design a grant application and review process—none of which I, or others, had done before. So, we immersed ourselves in learning and when we had questions, we asked experts in the community for help.

Glenda, was especially resourceful and enticed a local nonprofit guru to lunch so we could share our idea with him and pick his brain. It was important to get some feedback on our mission, our bylaws, and our approach from a leader in the Austin community.

She identified Barry Silverberg, Director of the Center for Nonprofit Studies at Austin Community College, as just the person to help us. Barry remembers his first contact with Impact Austin.

"A phone call from Glenda inviting me to lunch. I was traveling back from Dallas and stopped by an Arby's in Waco to take the call. I recall being impressed by the idea, but skeptical that it would reach fruition. At that point, I had not met you two and had not experienced your determination and passion to do good. You all created a valuable entity. I am grateful to have played a small part in the process."

Glenda and I still smile when thinking about that lunch we had with Barry. We proudly showed him a draft of our bylaws and asked for feedback. Ceremoniously, he took the cap off of his fountain pen and proceeded to mark up those bylaws—not a little—A LOT. His comments and edits made us think, and we continued to learn from him as Impact Austin matured. He's proud of us, and that's saying a lot—he's a tough cookie who doesn't lavish unwarranted praise.

At the end of our lunch, he suggested that we talk to Fayruz Benyousef, a successful fundraising consultant in town. She graciously agreed to meet me for coffee, offering some valuable feedback and made a few more introductions that helped us gain traction.

Reminiscing about our first meeting, she said, "I recall being blown away by your effusive energy and was inspired by your BIG plan that became Impact Austin. I remember thinking that your egalitarian approach and intent to engage women with the same level investment was so refreshing. And the combination of education for members about what nonprofits are doing and giving an "impact gift" was so needed in the community. I encouraged you to 'do it and don't stop,' and wanted our Association of Fundraising Professionals (AFP) to connect with your work. You got involved with AFP in a big way and became a trusted and revered member, major investor and advisor to the Chapter."

Barry and Fayruz mentored us unselfishly from the get-go when we were unknowns and continue to cheerlead for us today. I feel blessed to count them as friends, too.

With all of these Impact Austin start-up activities, I didn't have a predictable schedule. If the kids needed transportation to school and other activities, I expected Phil to pick up the slack. After all, I had been a devoted mom 24/7 to Brad and Claire when Phil was traveling the world for business. So, I didn't see this temporary need for him to step in and help with the kids as a huge imposition—especially as a newly retired person. One day in exasperation, I said, "I don't think you respect my devotion to Impact Austin because it doesn't bring income into the house."

He replied, "Reb, Impact Austin is a choice, not a job. You are choosing it over Brad, Claire and me."

That stung, and I went out on the back deck with my bruised ego and made friends with the same barn swallow that constantly flits across our deck railing. For some reason, he kept his gaze on me, so I asked him, "Am I really being as selfish as Phil says? Does anyone see how happy I am in the good work I am doing? Does anybody care? Does anybody remember the sacrifices I made when Phil was traveling the world for business?"

That barn swallow kept looking at me, and I felt him staring right into my soul. "Woman, what are you doing? Why are you compromising your family for this? Would your brother be proud of you?"

I don't think I really realized that I was giving up my family for my new venture, and it wasn't my intention. I hadn't even given it a thought that I would be forsaking my familial duties and how hard it would be for Phil to see this happening. And, no, Peter would not be proud of me.

Regularly, I shut the door to the spare bedroom which was my office and talked on the phone with other board members or sent emails well past our normal bedtime. I had another lover, and it was Impact Austin. I had never been part of something that excited me like this. For the first time since college, I felt daring and invincible. I had courage and attitude and limitless energy. I found alternate routes around obstacles in quick fashion. I was developing plans for my future, and it felt right to me but not to my family. I took them for granted, and they let me know they didn't like how my priorities had shifted.

One day in high school, Brad excitedly declared, "Mom, I get to start at shortstop when we play in the conference tournament coming up. Are you coming to the first game? If you have something with Impact Austin, I guess I understand. I just hope you don't."

Claire ventured, "Mom, my girlfriends and I want to go to the movies, and we need one more mom to drive us. Can you be that mom? I know you are really busy, but I thought I'd ask anyway."

Phil's devotion to all of us showed in his reactions. "Reb, I am worried that you're losing sight of what's most important. I want you to feel fulfilled, and I can see your joy. I'm just looking for balance for each of us. You and I will weather this chapter of life together, regardless. I just don't want you to miss the kids' special moments that you will never get back."

Sadly, it fell on deaf ears, and I continued to soldier on.

3

KITCHEN TABLE SIX

"A team is not a group of people who work together. A team is a group of people who trust each other."

-Mandala Principles

Glenda entered my life in 2001 at a neighborhood Bible study that a friend and I started a year earlier. At the beginning, my friend and I realized that so many of us were polite acquaintances, but we didn't really **know** each other. We took a leap of faith, put a plan in place and hand delivered invitations to about sixty neighbors to come to an informational coffee to learn more about the Bible study and to sign up if they wanted to participate. Twenty women joined that day, and twenty years later it is still going strong with eighty plus women involved from a multitude of neighborhoods. Clearly, there is something about starting new initiatives that feeds my soul.

Glenda attended the Bible study regularly and always had something positive to say. I could tell she was a "thinker," someone who absorbed information, chewed on it for a while and then shared her perspective after careful thought. I was intrigued by her style because it was so different from mine. At the time, I was the leader of our small group of ten, and I appreciated how willing she was to share her insecurities, her questions about God's grace and her desire to adopt a second child. As a group, we experienced the highs and lows of the adoption process through her eyes. It ended joyfully with the arrival of her little girl.

I stopped by a couple of weeks later with a baby gift: an engraved cake knife that her child could use for cutting all of the special cakes in her future. It's a family tradition my mother started with her grandchildren, and I've continued it with friends as babies have come into the world. It reminded me of when I brought Brad home from the hospital and then Claire a couple years later. I felt overwhelmed with the responsibility of raising these precious little humans. My childhood had been filled with too much discipline and not enough love, and I was determined to change that. Holding that little girl and seeing the love in Glenda's eyes made me wonder what her hopes and dreams were for her children and if I had been a good mom in the way I had dreamed. That seemed like an odd thought, but I let it pass and returned to focusing on this moment of joy.

The following year, I welcomed Glenda into my small group again. We created the groups from a blind draw, and I know God placed her there, but at the time I didn't know why. Upon my return from California, I shared my airplane experience with the group and the overwhelming feeling I had that I was supposed to start a women's philanthropy group in Austin. Glenda came up to me immediately following our group discussion and said, "I know some people who might be willing to help you get started, and I'd like to be one of your first investors." I was blown away. Another indication that I **had** to act on this inspiration! She and I decided to meet for coffee to talk about it some more.

The coffeehouse we chose was teeming with energy. A steady stream of customers flowed in and out. All of the tables in the place were occupied. Some with groups crowded around a table meant to hold far fewer. Some with single occupants working on laptops with earphones in their ears to drown out the constant chatter around them. After a short wait, we found a table for two and dove right in getting to know each other.

I started with, "Glenda, tell me something I don't know about you yet."

"Let's see, I moved from Florida to Austin as a young adult and married a Texan. We both graduated from UT and we've been in Austin ever since. Oh, and I'm a news junkie. I like to keep up on current events, and when I read something I don't know much about, I can easily get lost on the internet as I try to learn more."

She also shared her professional background. "I ran a business unit of a software company before retiring to stay home with my children, and I know a few women who might be interested in getting involved with Impact Austin." Later, as she recruited some of her past co-workers, I learned from them that she was smart, well-liked and fun.

Then, she asked me, "Have you started a business before? How do you create a 501(c)3 non-profit? I guess you need bylaws and a defined mission. How will you get operating capital?"

Her questions made me realize she had a lot of interest and that she'd be a great partner in this endeavor. Since she had already committed to pay the $1000 membership, I figured she might want to weigh in on how we put Impact Austin together too.

So, I posed the question, "Would you like to join the board and help me build this organization?"

She eagerly replied, "I think I do!"

As we started working together, we quickly discovered our similarities and differences. She reads lots of newspapers online and shares her findings with others on just about any topic. She is truly a living/breathing resource library. Contrast that with my penchant for reading *People* and romance novels and, at the time, my relative unfamiliarity with the internet, having just recently upgraded from Juno to AOL as my email provider.

When I make decisions, I trust my gut. Glenda prefers facts and figures to back up hers. She is quieter and more reserved, and I am more gregarious. In a crowd, Glenda gets to know a few people really well. I, on the other hand, make it a point to meet everyone in the room before I can call it a night. As time went on, I noticed I recognized a lot of members and knew their names, but I didn't get to know them. Really know them. So, I relied on Glenda's point of view often when considering which members we might engage in certain aspects of the organization. We made a great team that way.

We agreed so much of the time when making decisions that the few times we differed, I got testy and defensive. As the leader of the organization, I erroneously thought I always had to be right. Ultimately, the combination of our two styles served us well, even though I would often get impatient during the decision-making process. One time, I blurted out, "Glenda, we will never have all of the information we need to make this decision, but we have to act based on what we know." I think the honeymoon phase ended with that sentence! Though, our deep friendship continues to this day.

That neighborhood Bible study yielded another board member quite unexpectedly. Phylis and I first met volunteering at our kids' middle school in 1999. She and I both signed up to man the school supplies barn in the cafeteria one lunch hour per month. We didn't meet each other until our first shift together because we had each decided to take pot luck and hoped to meet someone new rather than teaming up with a friend. Bingo! We bonded instantly.

She had an effervescent personality that was like a magnet. Funny. Positive thinker. Sports enthusiast. Resourceful. Knew everyone. I mean everyone! And just a year or two older than I was—so we had fun joking about her maturity and my youth. She told great stories that kept us in stitches. We didn't try to impress each other. We were authentic from the get-go, and our friendship progressed quickly.

We brought "fast food takeout" for our kids on the days we volunteered. That was a huge status thing for our kids and made us feel needed and loved. We all know middle schoolers are very short on showing appreciation and affection to their parents. But, they had to come to the barn to get the goods. And, we brought extra food which meant their friends would stop by, too. So, everybody won. Phylis had a daughter a year younger than my son; so our friendship, as quickly as it grew, went dormant after our year of volunteering because our kids went in different directions, and well—life happens.

Then, out of the blue Phylis showed up in 2000 at our first-ever neighborhood Bible study kick-off coffee. We celebrated our reunion with hugs, smiles and laughter. I was so excited she came. I had no idea what her spiritual background was, but I knew she'd bring fun and joy to the study. In fact, I found out later that she was a bit worried we'd be too churchy or dogmatic, but in the spirit of being a good neighbor, she wanted to meet other women in our area and thought she'd give it a try.

In the fall of 2002, Phylis was put in my small group, and our bond really started to grow. She was so real and used spicy language if it helped her make a point. She shared her failings and her views with an ease and an honesty that made me want to learn more about her. She posed really thoughtful questions—the tough ones that didn't have one right answer. They always made us think. Soon, we all began to feel comfortable in our imperfectness because she was so willing to share hers.

As I was driving home from that Bible study after having told the group about Peter's sad prognosis and my compulsion to start Impact Austin, I realized I was following Phylis up the steep hill into our neighborhood. It sounds silly now, but I envisioned the hill as a mountain, and I saw both of us climbing it together as a team. In a flash, I knew I had to ask her if she wanted to help me grow this organization and called her when I got home. "Phylis, would you ever consider joining Impact Austin and…?"

Before I could blurt out the full invitation, she said, "Yes! I was planning to call you because this sounds like something that's right up my alley."

I knew having her on the team would help keep optimism high even in the midst of challenges. She had lots of friends she could invite to join, and she wanted to be our board Secretary—whew! Phylis worked quickly on any assignment. I learned I could trust her to do what she said she was going to do, and we could have honest conversations when that was necessary. Early on, I had no idea how to lead. Surrounding myself with people who shared my views was important. I didn't realize that respectful disagreements and brainstorming were healthy and brought better outcomes. I thought it meant I didn't know what I was doing. I believed if I didn't have all the answers, I couldn't gain everyone's respect.

Phylis was gentle and knew how to approach difficult situations with me. In hindsight, she played the role of sanity-checker. It was not a formal role, but one that played a huge part in helping me mature as a leader. She'd tell me when to push and when to hold back. When to weigh in and when to be silent. She taught me how to laugh at myself, which has come in handy over the years. Our connection continues to grow deeper to this day. We walk together regularly and check in on each other via email. It's not unusual for either of us to end a note with LYLAS which stands for "love you like a sister."

Glenda, Phylis and I each agreed to invite someone we thought would make a great addition to our board. We had different circles of friends, and that was critical when thinking about finding one hundred women to invest in our idea.

By the time we held our first meeting in March, we had added Cindy to the board. She and I first met at a community Bible study, and our sons played high school baseball together. As we sat in the stands watching a baseball game that February (baseball starts early in Texas), I told her about Impact Austin and how much fun I was having forming a team to lead it. We had bundled up in blankets, wearing mittens and stocking caps to keep warm, and the conversation provided a nice diversion. Her beautiful Texas drawl, with occasional "y'alls" thrown in, made it fun for me. I still cannot get enough of that accent. The more we talked, the more animated I grew and the more interested she became.

So, I took a leap of faith and asked if she'd like to invest $1000 and help build the organization. She said, "Yes!" immediately, and I was thrilled—gaining more confidence every time I shared the idea. Cindy's husband had started a non-profit a few years earlier and knew the expenses we'd incur. So, he gave us a generous contribution to help defray some of our start-up costs. Things were falling into place nicely, reminding me the wind beneath my cape was not my own.

For that March meeting, I prepared a simple lunch of finger sandwiches filled with homemade chicken salad, fresh veggies and dip and 4-H brownies that I'd been baking since sixth grade. I wanted these women to know how much I appreciated their commitment, and making lunch was one way of showing my gratitude. Nervous excitement filled the air as the hour for the meeting approached. There were so many ideas running through my head; so many unknowns. I had been president of my kids' elementary PTA in the mid-'90s, but that was the extent of my previous board experience. I had no idea what to expect. What if we disagreed on an important issue? Would we get along, regardless? None of us knew each other well enough to know how we'd interact. Could we be serious about getting the work done and still have fun in the process? Would everyone still be as excited after our first meeting as they were before it started?

Before everyone arrived, I lovingly set the dining room table with the carefully ironed linen tablecloth Peter had given me six months earlier. In early 2002, Peter visited Vietnam to meet a woman he had been corresponding with over the internet for more than a year. She was his "princess" and the love of his life. He had saved and saved in order to take the trip. Even though some in our family did not approve of this long-distance internet romance with a much younger woman, Peter showed his resolve in pursuing her and deepening his involvement with her. While I had reservations about her motivation for accepting Peter's love, I just listened when he talked about her and told him I could feel the smile in his voice over the phone. Clearly, she made my brother happy, and that's what mattered to me.

Peter bought my mother, sister and me each a beautifully hand-stitched linen tablecloth while in Vietnam. He presented them to us at my parents' fiftieth wedding anniversary celebration, delighting in our smiles and appreciation as we unwrapped our gifts. He was so proud of what he had chosen, and I was very touched by his generosity. I ceremoniously iron out the professional creases from the dry cleaners before each use—knowing that Peter is enjoying every moment of this careful practice in honor of him. I can see that mischievous twinkle in his eye reminding me he's my big brother, and he is still making me do things on his behalf.

Phylis arrived first and spoke with an urgency that made you think the fire was about to reach our street. Her bright, cheery disposition lit up the room. Cindy arrived next, and immediately introduced herself to Phylis. Cindy was more reserved, but so excited to be part of the founding board and ready to take on whatever tasks she was assigned. As Cindy and Phylis spoke to each other and talked about their mutual enthusiasm for the project, Glenda came through the front door and introductions began again.

Glenda showed up with lots of questions and ideas—an attribute we came to appreciate over time because she could look at a situation from many angles. She played devil's advocate often, which helped us make better decisions. We knew when it was coming because she would remove her glasses, cock her head and scrunch her nose right before she started in. Again, I figured it was my job as the leader to have all of the answers and do whatever it took to get everyone to accept my views. Needless to say, we had some contentious discussions in subsequent board meetings that could have been diffused had I understood the importance of listening and building consensus!

The four of us sat around my dining room table as I shared the significance of the tablecloth and that Peter was with us in spirit. You could hear a pin drop, and tears flowed freely. Little did he know when he gave it to me that it would have a specific purpose and forever be known as the Impact Austin tablecloth. It reminded us that we had all come together as a team to create good from tragedy, and we had a powerful silent partner. I continued to use the tablecloth for special Impact Austin gatherings and always got a warm feeling knowing Peter was present. I know others did, too.

We already had a name for our organization and a book that would help us get started in forming our 501(c)(3) non-profit. Phylis took notes. She was efficient with words and captured conversations accurately and concisely. We were spoiled from the get-go, and I missed her skills when she moved to another position on the board.

The collective enthusiasm of our foursome made it hard to stay on track as our conversation went from topic to topic. How will we recruit members? What will our grant application and review process look like? Who will open the bank account? How do we file the necessary legal documents to form a 501(c)3 non-profit? Each of us took responsibility for certain tasks, and we agreed to meet the following month to report on our progress.

I knew things had gone well because we all hugged each other at the end of the meeting, and there was genuine appreciation flowing as the hugs lingered longer than one might expect after an initial meeting like this. Shortly after that first meeting, Nancy and Jane joined, which completed the board.

Glenda introduced me to Nancy over lunch at a local salad bar. When Nancy smiled, her eyes sparkled, and our conversation flowed easily. We sat in a booth with Glenda on one side and Nancy and me on the other. That way, Glenda could make eye contact and read Nancy's body language as she shared the Impact Austin idea. Glenda and she had been co-workers, and their mutual respect for each other came through in the first few minutes of conversation. They reminisced easily, sharing fun stories and catching up on mutual friends.

Nancy had just taken a leave of absence on her way to eventual retirement, and she hadn't figured out what she was going to do with her free time yet. She commented that while she had lived in Austin for years, she didn't really know much about her community because she was constantly living out of a suitcase traveling across the country for work. Glenda capitalized on that and talked about the fun we were having putting Impact Austin together.

Before Glenda could finish, Nancy agreed to join the board. While I had just met Nancy, it was easy to welcome her to the team because I trusted Glenda. Nancy soon became our one-person marketing department. Her son, an amateur photographer, had taken a close-up picture of a scrub daisy in their backyard, which provided the inspiration for our logo. Nancy created our first brochure in her home office and invested in whatever hardware and software she needed to get the job done. She was like a wizard behind a black curtain who magically produced amazing marketing collateral and absorbed all of the associated costs. For the first few years, she provided all of our printing needs, which was a huge contribution of time and dollars.

Nancy also brought lots of new members into the fold over the years. It was hard to resist her charm. Most of her neighbors invested, which demonstrated the trust they had in her. If she was involved, they wanted to be a part of it, too. She also got her female relatives to join, even if they didn't live in Austin. Her generosity exploded as she learned about non-profits doing great things in the community, and she gave liberally to the ones that addressed issues she cared about. Impact Austin has been a springboard for many women to find their voices and use them for good. Nancy has been a great example of that.

Jane came to Impact Austin via her connection with Phylis. Their daughters were high school classmates, and Phylis had served on some committees with Jane. So, she knew Jane's strengths first-hand. The three of us had lunch, and Jane immediately agreed to join and serve on the board. I remember when she gave her first report at a board meeting. She had created PowerPoint slides, and it intimidated me because I was not tech-savvy. She worked for a large computer technology company and used that software all the time. She encouraged me to embrace it, and I realized I could learn a lot from her. She also brought lots of ideas to the table as we agonized over our mission, vision and values early on.

While we rotated houses between the six of us for our board meetings, we soon realized that each time we met it was around someone's kitchen table. There was something very grounding about that, and it bonded us. Everyone had a kitchen table, which was a great equalizer. We had no idea how important that would be as Impact Austin grew. It serves as a reminder as to where it all started and that kitchen tables do not mean you cannot be professional and impactful. It means you are resourceful and use the tools you have to create your masterpiece. Over the years our founding board has been lovingly dubbed The Kitchen Table Six, and we wear that title proudly.

I normally cultivated friendships with women who thought like I did, were fun to be around and didn't challenge my thinking. In fact, I was known for being happy, optimistic and confident. I always had my act together and showed genuine interest in what was going on in my friends' lives. My house was always clean, and I could host a meeting or social gathering at a moment's notice. My kids were well-behaved and good students. If you asked me to help out, I consistently said "yes" and overachieved—no matter what the task. I was (and still am) very much in love with my husband and said so publicly. I had a reputation for being very persuasive, thanks to the stellar sales training I received at IBM back in the '70s. I was well-liked, which has been important to me my entire life. In fact, my friends told me I was a great leader.

I said, "No, not true."

They said, "Of course you are!"

And so it went. Eventually, I began to believe it in some small way.

I had been out of the traditional workforce for thirteen years by 2003. I had never managed people—I just knew how to sell ideas, business or otherwise. Instinctively, I knew the Impact Austin board needed women who thought strategically, honored deadlines, and easily voiced their opinions as we made pivotal decisions regarding the business.

I had no idea how many approaches to a single issue could surface during a brainstorming session. My approach to collective decision-making was simple: ask for everyone's input, sell everyone on my viewpoint and wait until they all agreed with me. I mistakenly believed that a good leader could convince anyone of anything, and that it was my job to do that no matter what the cost. Painfully and often, I found my approach did not work well. "Because I am the founder" is not particularly effective with adults, and I should have known better. "Because I'm your mom" didn't work with my kids either. But, it's all I knew. I didn't have the leadership tools to deal with divergent views and was called out on my need to control situations. Alliances formed out of my view, and I would be double-teamed at board meetings.

Mentally exhausted and feeling a bit numb after one board meeting, I went out to the deck, and the barn swallow showed up. I needed to vent, and he was the perfect audience.

"Why am I such a control freak? I know it takes a team to make this dream work, and I keep sabotaging our efforts. Am I worried that people will let me down if I let go of some things just like some volunteers let me down when I was PTA President?"

He cocked his slate-blue head and looked at me, "Those are great questions that you have to answer. I'll sit here as long as it takes. You don't need to lose friendships over things like this. And, what if you started to trust that these women will hold up their end of the bargain? You are not giving them credit for having as much passion as you do."

Wow. I left the deck with some homework. And, I felt better just having taken the time to reflect on my feelings even if I didn't have ready answers.

I now hold fast to a quote from Jim Collins, author of *Good to Great and the Social Sectors*. "True leadership only exists if people follow when they have the freedom not to." I get that intellectually, but making sure my actions mirror my beliefs is a constant learning opportunity for me. Impact Austin largely accomplishes its mission through the volunteer efforts of its members, who take on lots of operational duties. I've learned that our members thrive when they are given clear guidelines and the freedom to execute as they see fit within those guidelines. They feel empowered and appreciated for their competencies and, in turn, deliver excellent results. They feel ownership in our success and continue to volunteer, which encourages others to get involved.

I am learning to be a better leader every day because I have people in my life that refine me. Sometimes it's painful. It's always helpful. My Impact Austin comrades keep me in line, and I get to practice my leadership skills continually. Our mutual respect makes that possible.

I've learned that saying "I don't know" is a perfectly acceptable response to a question. It took me a long time to feel comfortable as the leader not being the one with all the answers. I've also learned that perfect and good enough are important distinctions to make when assessing what's necessary with a given project. Perfect is important when sending out a newsletter that reflects our brand.

Typos and misspellings are not acceptable. Good enough works when writing board reports. The format doesn't matter as long as the content is accurate. As a recovering perfectionist, I'm proud of myself for seeing the value in good enough now.

I realize now that Peter's death propelled me headlong into a journey of self-discovery. The good, bad and ugly all revealed themselves. I'm learning to embrace it all, and I am **mostly** grateful for the lessons I'm learning.

From time to time during my leadership tenure, I wrote blogs I never published. They are sprinkled throughout this book and reveal my heart at different points along the journey. Here is one of them.

Leader in the Cornfield

As a young teenager, I excitedly signed up to detassel corn. For a 14-year old kid living in Morton, IL, in the late '60s, the pay was fabulous. The work was grueling. For days on end, I would climb into one of six 'buckets' attached to the side of a tractor that moved slowly through a field of 6' tall cornstalks. My job was to pull the tassel from each stalk of corn I passed without missing a single one. The tractor driver sat much higher than those of us in the buckets, and he could see which tassels we missed. The tractor stopped and started all day long as, one by one, we'd each miss a tassel. We'd have to get out of our buckets and walk to the stalk we missed, bend its top down and pull out the tassel. We had to get every single one, or the tractor driver got in trouble.

The first day was awful. The tractor driver lectured us and yelled at us out of frustration, knowing he was accountable for any missed tassels. We all felt the pressure and began to feel like we couldn't succeed. The second day, we had a different driver, and we were prepared for the same admonishments from him, but that was not to be. The 'substitute' driver was clever. He started out encouraging us to do our best and praised us for doing a great job along the way. Not surprisingly, we had fewer misses, and we started feeling more confident. He also realized that by driving just a 'teensy' slower than the dictated speed, we could detassel more effectively without having to stop as often and pull the missed ones manually. That meant our detasseling crew got out of the hot sun sooner, and we were all on speaking terms by the end of the day. Every detasseler wanted to be in this driver's crew because the day went smoother and the mood was lighter. Always.

I have never forgotten that tractor driver. The task we faced each day was the same. Our effectiveness depended on the leadership skills of the driver. I don't know what that 'substitute' driver is doing today, but I'd gladly work for him. He was absolutely brilliant! Would those that work with me say the same thing? I'm being called to attention, and I'm listening.

As founding board members, the six of us had two things in common: various business backgrounds and **no** understanding of the nonprofit landscape in Austin. We knew the names of very few non-profits in our community, and none of us had made donations in any significant way to local causes. Thankfully, our corporate backgrounds helped us when it came to creating both the business model and a business plan to accomplish our goals.

The model was simple: each member invests $1000 annually by December 31, and all of it goes to the grant pool. The first week in January, we announce to the nonprofit community how many grants we will extend the following June and for how much. Non-profits apply for the grants; finalists are chosen; and each member gets one vote to determine the grant recipients.

While the concept was easy to understand, the fair execution of the grant application and review process was more complex and needed lots of checks and balances in order to protect the integrity of the one woman-one vote structure. Every member was invited to sit on one of several grant review committees, which required mandatory training. The review process itself took place over a 5-month period with a few meetings and plenty of personal time for committee members to carefully review and evaluate applications, using a rubric that made the process consistent across all committees. In the end, each committee recommended a finalist. These finalists made written and oral presentations to our members, and the winner was chosen via secret ballot with each member casting one vote.

I remember one committee member, who served on a grant review committee our first year, stating proudly, "As a retired elementary school teacher, I felt like I'd been put on a shelf, and this experience has shown me that I'm smart and capable. I can now read a non-profit's financial statements without being intimidated because of the training Impact Austin has given me."

Glenda spent hundreds of hours developing the grant application and review process by learning best practices in that arena. She recruited another founding member to help her build out the process and also to help create the training program for our members who sat on grant review committees. They delivered spectacular results, and to this day, Impact Austin uses much of what they created—a testimony to their thorough understanding of what makes the process fair and equitable.

Our family's small house on Lake Travis provided the perfect setting for our first board retreat, and Glenda came out the night before to set up and help me prepare. I brought groceries to make the food and snacks we'd have on Saturday. She agreed to facilitate the meeting and wanted to get organized so that we could be really productive. I loved the company, and we enjoyed spending uninterrupted time together that night brainstorming. In fact, we had so much to share that we stayed up way too late just talking.

"Reb, let's think about the setup here. How do we make it comfortable for everyone? I have some flipcharts and post-it notes to help move things along tomorrow, and I have an agenda that should get us to a good place by the end of the day."

"I'm so glad you are facilitating. That is not my strength, and I feel really good with you leading us through the retreat. How can I help you?"

"You can make sure that everyone gets the chance to speak up. I'll leave it to you to encourage the quieter ones to weigh in. Though, I'm not sure that's something we have to worry about with this crowd."

Our conversation eventually turned personal, and we talked about our childhoods. What we did for fun. How our kids were doing. The longer we talked, the more comfortable we became opening up to each other. I can't remember all of the things we discussed. I just know it got easier with each passing hour to go deeper and talk about feelings…not just surface stuff.

Everyone arrived on Saturday for breakfast, and we did some ice breakers. Lots of laughter and silliness blended with a real desire to get to know and trust each other…especially since we would be spending lots of time together over the next several months building Impact Austin. At lunchtime, I brought out champagne as we toasted to excellence and celebrated our progress.

Here we were, sitting around yet another kitchen table bouncing ideas around. We refined our words continually until we finalized our mission statement. Our tagline was a little harder to come by, but when it came to us, we *loved* it and embraced it by saying it over and over again to each other: "Ordinary Women—Extraordinary Impact." The more we said it, the more we believed it. We all felt ownership in the final result, and that beautiful display of teamwork set the tone for our success as a board and an organization. While the mission statement and tagline have evolved over the years, we have held fast to the warm and welcoming culture we established from the start.

When the retreat ended, I collapsed in tears feeling emotionally exhausted and checked in with Glenda as I tried to dry them. "Do you think the retreat went well?" She was surprised at my question; it was the first time she'd seen my confident exterior dissolve.

"We accomplished so much today, and everyone left feeling good about our progress. I hope you feel good about that, too."

Somehow that satisfied me, and my frame of mind improved. She possessed skills we needed—ones I didn't have. I felt a bit insecure and didn't understand at the time that good leaders surround themselves with people like Glenda who are smarter than they are.

I also realized the enormity of what lay ahead. It was time to start executing on our well-developed business plan, and it overwhelmed me momentarily. Glenda had graciously walked me through my emotions, which strengthened our connection even more. It was "go time" and I got on with our plan.

4

MAKING THE CASE

You always have the power; you just need to know
where to find it."

—Frances Hesselbein,
CEO Girl Scouts of the USA

As new grantmakers, we had much to learn. We devoted lots of time to acquiring knowledge about our community and fair grantmaking practices. We taught ourselves and then taught our members. We role modeled effective facilitation practices for the committee leaders. We encouraged questions and suggestions. Every voice mattered—whether we agreed, or not. We believed if we built a sense of sisterhood within the organization first, we could serve Central Texas better.

Though we did not set out to create a model of servant leadership in the community, it is what Impact Austin is known for. Our members are our volunteers, and they are also our investors. Making sure each member feels valued helps those of us in leadership adjust our priorities accordingly. We have successfully created an organized capacity to care for one another. Not just member to member, but leader to member, and member to community.

As Glenda continued to research women's collective giving, she learned of Sondra Shaw-Hardy and Martha Taylor, co-founders of the Women's Philanthropy Institute. They had developed the "Six C's of Women's Philanthropic Giving." Create. Change. Connect. Collaborate. Commit. Celebrate. We shared these six C's at recruiting coffees and how we wove each into our mission, culture and processes. It lent credibility to our young organization before we had made our first grant. Thanks to Glenda's efforts, we started strong!

At our first recruiting coffee, we shared the Impact Austin story with twenty-four women. We chose them carefully, thinking they could write a $1000 check, but we didn't know for sure. And, since they were known to us, we hoped if they decided not to make a membership pledge, they'd be kind in their declination. After the women assembled, I went to the front of the room, took a deep breath and started to share our story. Tears formed in my eyes and seemingly came from nowhere. I stopped and composed myself with the help of Peter sitting on my shoulder and continued with the presentation. I ended by saying we wanted to extend our first grant on Peter's birthday, June 12, the following year. The room was silent. Some women had tears in their eyes; others came and gave me a hug. They understood that Impact Austin was not going to be a shrine to my brother, but that its success would honor his memory.

After returning from the gathering that night, I read the response cards. All but one attendee committed to join! From that moment on, I knew we would find the other women we needed in order to extend our first $100,000 grant. Overwhelmed with emotion, I cried for the second time that night. But, these were tears of joy. I knew, without a single doubt, Impact Austin would help heal the hole in my heart and went to sleep feeling encouraged and determined—with determination leading the way.

By the way, "coffee" is a misnomer. We hold our recruitment gatherings in the evening and normally serve wine. While we've agonized for years over finding a different name for this function, we haven't come up with anything better. Calling it a "wine" doesn't work, but serving wine does. It's amazing how receptive attendees are when holding a glass of cabernet. They can see themselves as grantmakers having fun while making a difference.

I still laugh out loud when I think about one of our first coffees. I explained that members could be as involved or uninvolved as they chose. There were no volunteer requirements and no special favors granted to members who volunteered more than others. That statement prompted a woman in the back to stand up and address me, "Young lady, I am a tired grandmother, and I will join because there is no volunteer requirement. But, if you ask me to bake **one** cookie, I will not renew my membership. If you leave me alone, I will come to the Annual Meeting in June and give you my $1000 check for next year." We kept our promise to her, and she kept hers to us.

As we ramped up our recruiting efforts, I asked Impact 100 in Cincinnati if I could attend their second annual meeting scheduled for that October. Our first annual meeting was several months away, and I wanted to get a bird's eye view as to how they showcased their grant finalists, how their members voted and what the flow of the annual meeting looked like. Enthusiastically, they obliged and also set up a time for me to visit the dental clinic that received their first grant.

The combination of my attendance at Impact 100's annual meeting and my visit to the dental clinic the next day galvanized me. To see over one hundred women come together to vote and celebrate the results when not everyone's first choice won; to have the dentist at the clinic tell me, "We don't give our homeless patients back their smiles, we give them back their lives." It hit me that the impact is far greater than the $100,000 grant itself. I was so focused on the money that I hadn't considered the human aspect.

Now, I had a vision of the lives we would impact—not only of those who received our funds, but the lives of our members, too. Women, whose hearts would be forever changed just as mine was when I set foot in that dental clinic. I returned to Austin with a story to tell at our recruiting coffees, helping women to visualize the possibilities that lay ahead for Impact Austin.

Early in our recruiting efforts, Phylis and I attended the monthly Association of Fundraising Professionals luncheon as Fayruz had encouraged us to do. We didn't know what to expect and felt a bit nervous, but by going together, we felt bolder. We sat at a table for eight and told our story about starting Impact Austin and what our goals were. A well-respected fundraising consultant in our city heard about our plan, followed us out of the luncheon and said flatly, "Whatever you do, don't tell any of the boards I consult with what you are doing. Your approach never works. Besides, I've never met a group of one hundred women who can agree on anything."

I locked eyes with him and said, "Sir, I want you to remember two things: the name Impact Austin and June 12, 2004, when we will give our first $100,000 grant." He looked at me and nodded skeptically. Phylis and I couldn't wait to get to the car and "dis" that man. Here we were, new to philanthropy and not being taken seriously. We made a pact to prove that man wrong, and we did!

November and December whizzed by. Phylis and I traveled around town as a team and shared the Impact Austin story with groups of women, inviting them to jump on the bandwagon and invest. On the side, she and I started a contest to see who could bring in the most members personally. We had so much fun challenging each other to find just one more member. I kept a messy, handwritten list of who brought whom into Impact Austin. Other board members got a bit jealous of our contest and wanted to know how many they'd brought in, too. In the end, it served the organization well to have this competition. Though, no one came close to the individual recruiting success that Phylis and I enjoyed—mostly because it was our sole job that fall. And, it was important that she and I take the lead and take it seriously.

Because we knew some of the same women that joined and had both spoken to them, we occasionally argued about who got credit for a specific recruit.

"Hey, Reb, Mary just said she'd join. Put her name on my side of the ledger. One more for me. Once you've done that, give me the tally to date. I'm pumped!"

Playfully, I replied, "Phylis, I talked to Mary, too. I think you should only get half credit for her. Besides, I think Mary likes me better."

Phylis retorted, "If that's the way this game is going to be played, I'm only going to talk to women you don't know. This is war."

Our repartee amused us, and neither of us gave up the hunt for one more member.

We met at the local Mexican restaurant occasionally and pumped each other up over a margarita with chips and salsa. By the time we left, we each had a new list of women to approach. We dared each other to be the first to convert one of the prospects on our list to a member. That competitive aspect of our friendship made those first uncertain months lots of fun. And, we learned a lot about each other along the way. She likes salt on her margarita glass. I don't. I tear up faster than she does, but we both cry easily. She is a diehard University of Texas fan, and I am not. But knowing her loyalty to UT, and considering we live in Austin, TX, I keep my fondness for Big 10 schools to myself and avoid many unnecessary arguments.

As December arrived and we hadn't reached our membership goal, doubt crept in. As I pulled up to the Mail Store to make some last-minute copies for an upcoming meeting, Sarah McLachlan's "Angel" started playing on the radio. I had not heard that song since Peter's memorial service when it had moved me to uncontrollable sobbing. While jarring and eerie at first, I put the car in park and sat with my eyes closed as I saw my brother smiling at me, telling me to "breathe" to "believe" and to "trust." In less than the five minutes it took to listen to the song, my heart eased and my confidence returned. Two other songs remind me of my brother, and they come on the radio at the most unbelievable times—just when I need a boost of energy or a stress release.

Peter has never really left me. He's just in a different form now as my personal angel.

Heading home from my errand, I was greeted by a sight that made me smile and prompted this blog, which still makes me grin.

Tinsel, anyone?

I was driving along Capital of Texas Highway today and had already started making a mental to-do list as my mind turned toward the week ahead. As the list grew, so did my heart rate. A lot to clean up from this year's Thanksgiving weekend and so much more to accomplish before Christmas arrived.

Turning off the highway, my eyes caught a glimpse of Christmas decorations on 'orphan' cedar trees growing on the side of the road. About forty of them. Nondescript for eleven months out of the year. Until Thanksgiving weekend when dozens of families, couples and groups of friends adopt and painstakingly decorate these trees. Every year. Like clockwork. I couldn't resist the urge to pull off the road and take in the beautiful handiwork. The trees looked regal with their tinsel-draped limbs. Ornaments of all shapes and sizes graced the tree branches from top to bottom. It was a visual symphony, and I teared up—just like I do the first time I see them each holiday season as I'm reminded to s-l-o-w down and enjoy the next several weeks.

This day, a group of girlfriends was decorating one tree as a family of five decorated another. The smiles on their faces and the fun they were having were unmistakable. It made me smile, too. Before the day's end, I knew each tree would be adorned with just the right amount of garland, tinsel and ornaments by an unnamed group of people wanting to put smiles on the faces of strangers. Starting today, the view from the highway would give every rush hour driver a reason to take a deep breath and enjoy the season.

It doesn't take long to decorate these trees, and the ornaments, tinsel and garland don't have much monetary value, but that doesn't matter when it touches the hearts of thousands of drivers like me and reminds all of us to enjoy the season. When I got home, I rushed in the door to describe my experience in extreme detail to my husband. He cracked a knowing smile and reminded me how cool it is to live in Austin, TX. I couldn't agree more!

May your heart be merry and light, and may all your Christmases be bright!

At the end of December, I had edged Phylis out in recruiting—not by much, but she knew I would claim victory even if it involved cheating. Neither of us cared as long as Impact Austin met its goal, which we did in spades. We brought out the best in each other and together brought 126 women into Impact Austin.

Earlier that fall as we simultaneously recruited members and finalized our grant application/review process, I read an article in the newspaper about the Austin Area Human Services Association, a group of local nonprofit executive directors that met monthly to discuss issues their agencies faced and ways to support each other while advocating for their causes.

I reached out to one of the group's members and asked if they'd like to learn about the $100,000 grant we expected to extend the following June. We wanted to get them excited about the opportunity to apply and to get their help in spreading the word.

They graciously invited us to their October meeting and gave us ten minutes on the agenda.

We had prepared well and felt confident that we could get their interest and earn just a tiny bit of credibility. I spoke about our collective giving model and shared that we already had thirty-six of the one hundred members we expected to have by December 31. Glenda very clearly laid out the grant application process and timeline. We left the meeting feeling very positive and grateful for the opportunity to share our plans.

We learned later that while they were happy to see a group of women who might bring a new source of grant funding to the community, they remained skeptical because they didn't know us and we didn't have a track record. They also thought we were a bit too optimistic about our ability to find sixty-four more women to invest in our mission by year's end. It felt good to prove them wrong!

On January 6, 2004, we invited all non-profits in Central Texas to attend an information session in order to introduce ourselves and share our upcoming grant opportunity. Our friend, Barry Silverberg, arranged for us to use the local community college's board room for the announcement. Our invitation yielded 183 attendees, and that excited us. Word had definitely spread, and if nothing else, we created an atmosphere of curiosity.

We shared a PowerPoint slide presentation, which included the who, what, where, when and how of Impact Austin and a timeline for the application/review process. We also made handouts for the attendees to take back to their offices so they could start the application process immediately. We saved the best news for last and showed a slide that had a single number on it. $126,000. We had easily exceeded our publicly stated goal of $100,000—even though, behind the scenes, we wanted to reach $124,000 to surpass the $123,000 Impact 100 had raised in its first year.

When that final slide appeared, it made us proud because we had created a nonprofit organization and had raised $126,000 in less than nine months. It was a powerful moment in our young existence, and we all knew it was only the beginning of what Impact Austin would accomplish in the community going forward.

After showing the final slide, we asked for questions. Most of them concerned logistics and the deadline for applying, and some attendees told us how grateful they were for what we planned to do. We moved right along until a skeptical executive director with a high-profile non-profit, who was sitting near the front, asked two questions.

"Is that $126,000 just pledged or in the bank?"

The inquiry alerted us to the fact that we were the new kids on the block and trust in us and our process had to be earned. It felt good to say it was in the bank, though it never occurred to us to announce an amount that we didn't have in hand. The second question revealed even more skepticism.

"Do you think you women are really up to this?" I will never forget those piercing words. The tone was patronizing, and I immediately felt defensive as I experienced a huge rush of adrenaline to go with it.

I took a deep breath, smiled and calmly replied, "The only way you'll know the answer to that is to apply for our grant." Then, I immediately looked away and asked the audience, "Are there any other questions?" Impact Austin definitely established some credibility that morning, and our board left that meeting feeling great about Impact Austin's future.

On Friday, February 27, at 5 p.m., our inaugural grant application process closed. We had no idea how many applications to expect, and we were nervous that we might not get many in spite of offering a $126,000 grant opportunity. On Monday of that week, I placed a large plastic bin on my front porch with the Impact Austin logo carefully affixed to its lid. That way, as people dropped off their applications, they would know where to put them and the bin would keep them safe and dry. By Friday at noon, only two applications had arrived. Talk about disappointment!

Several board members came over that day to help with receiving the applications, but mostly to just share in the excitement of the moment. We used my dining room table for receiving the applications and established an organized system for recording what came in.

Phylis commented, "Well, this certainly isn't the celebration I expected."

"It's like having a party and putting all of the food out wondering if the doorbell will ever ring," lamented Cindy.

Nancy declared, "I'm not going to get all worked up about this yet. There are still several hours left before the deadline. Maybe they all come in at the last minute."

We kept pumping each other up as we looked at the empty table so as not to get depressed about the lack of activity at my front door. By 2 p.m., we received a few more applications, but it wasn't looking promising. Our plan to celebrate our success with champagne at 5:01 p.m. looked bleak until about 4:15 p.m. Then, things changed—oh, did they change!

The pace quickened as cars pulled up to the front curb. Board members took turns going out to retrieve the applications so that drivers didn't have to park their vehicles and deliver their packages to the front door. Initially, we saw it as a courtesy, and it gave us something to do. Quickly, courtesy changed to necessity. Cars came from all directions. It was sheer insanity. At one point, the street looked like a fast food drive-thru, and we delighted in that. We fielded various phone calls from people who had trouble finding my house. A courier called at 4:53 p.m. to say he was on his way with a delivery and was frantic thinking he might not meet the deadline. He knew he was close and pleaded with us to allow him to hand off the application if he was a few minutes late. Of course we said "yes." We appreciated the fact that applicants took the deadline seriously.

In total, we received eighty-seven applications—eighty-five of them between noon and 5 p.m. We realized the joke was on us. Of course most of the applications showed up right before the deadline! Nancy was right. That's how life works, and each of us recalled sliding in at the last minute to meet a deadline at some point in our own lives. We popped some champagne, patted ourselves on the back and cheered. The nonprofit community had offered eighty-seven different ideas for using $126,000.

Over seventy-five members participated on one of four grant review committees, ensuring that the applications were vetted by many different women with a wide variety of lived experiences and levels of expertise. We delighted in the fact that so many members wanted to participate in the review process because it showed their eagerness to learn and a desire to volunteer in a meaningful way.

Soon, my thoughts turned toward our first annual meeting. I wanted to create a tradition that honored my brother, recognizing one of his character traits by choosing a member who exhibited that same one. Since Peter was an accomplished bowler, I decided to give a bowling pin engraved with "For Pete's Sake" as the award. The idea came to me so easily that I knew it was solid. What I didn't know was where to find a new bowling pin that someone was willing to donate. I didn't have to look far....

In March, I joined the Rotary Club of Austin, which met at a downtown hotel. I exited the car feeling my self-confidence and outgoing personality take a hike as I wondered if anyone would talk to me. At that moment, two older men approached. One of them asked where I was going and let me know they were going to Rotary, too.

The other gentleman looked at me, rolled his eyes and said, "You might as well get to know Jerry. He owns all of the bowling alleys in town."

Music to my ears! My eyes lit up, and I replied, "Jerry, it's a pleasure to meet you, and we have some business to discuss."

Jerry leaned a little closer to me and said, "Sugar, come to Dart Bowling Center tomorrow afternoon and tell me what this is all about."

My feet didn't touch the ground the rest of that day. I had been dreading going to a bowling center to ask for a donation of a bowling pin. I didn't want to share my brother's story with a stranger as I would no doubt be fighting back tears, but I had pretty much resigned myself to the fact that I was going to have to do that.

At Jerry's office the next day, we exchanged pleasantries and small talk for about twenty minutes. He was a proud and active alumnus of Texas Christian University and sat on their Board of Trustees. His office was filled with TCU memorabilia, and he shared his excitement about his alma mater with me. When we got to a wall of family photos, he told me about his wife and two children. His daughter had died six years earlier, leaving behind a husband and two young sons. Tears formed in his eyes as he talked about her. Of course, that caused a chain reaction, and I started tearing up. Jerry was embarrassed that he'd made me cry about someone I didn't even know. Then, I confessed to him my reason for needing a bowling pin. Once he learned that I had lost my brother, it created a bond between our families that continues today.

Before leaving his office, he asked me about my children. I told him about Brad, our high school junior, who played varsity baseball and got good grades. Jerry only cared about the latter and asked what colleges Brad was considering. While I didn't know the complete list, I did know he was not interested in going to college in Texas.

Jerry looked at me, his eyes piercing mine like lasers, and pronounced, "I'd like to meet your son and talk to him. If nothing else, he needs to visit TCU to know why he's not considering a school in Texas. There's no pressure for him to attend TCU, but I'd like to take him up there to meet some people and see the campus before he ignores the opportunity."

I promised to ask Brad, with little hope of a positive response. To my surprise, Brad willingly accompanied me to meet Jerry several weeks later. He had enjoyed my story about meeting Jerry and figured it wouldn't hurt to know a smart businessman in town either. When we stepped into Jerry's office, a brand new bowling pin sat on his desk, awaiting our arrival. In telltale "Jerry style," as he saw me eyeing the pin, he told me that he was now Impact Austin's official bowling pin supplier. What an affirmation!

Jerry connected easily with teenagers and talked to lots of local high school students who were interested in TCU. It was a bit of a different story the day he met Brad. Here was a kid with no interest in TCU. And, did Jerry ever turn on the charm. He asked Brad all the right questions to learn more about him and the final one sealed Brad's fate.

"Brad, how about if I take you up to TCU in July and show you around and let you talk to some people about the school—just so you know for sure you don't want to go there."

Before Brad could reply, Jerry picked up his phone and dialed the TCU Chancellor's office to make an appointment for Brad to meet with him. Still not looking at Brad, but looking at me, Jerry directed me to pull my calendar out to confirm a date.

As I was doing that, he looked over at Brad and said, "Is this okay with you, Brad?"

Again, before Brad could answer, Jerry was talking to the Chancellor's assistant and making the appointment.

Brad looked at me, shrugged his shoulders and said, "I guess I'm going to visit TCU!"

Jerry drove Brad and me up and back to the campus one day in July. It was a whirlwind of activity, and each person with whom Brad spoke shared something about TCU that really piqued his interest. He could not get over the fact that the Chancellor had given him a half hour of his time to make him feel wanted. The tide was turning in Brad's mind. He did, in fact, apply and was accepted at TCU.

In August, 2005, Brad entered TCU with an academic scholarship given to a select group of students. And to think this all started because I needed a bowling pin. I tell the bowling pin story to a lot of audiences to show how Impact Austin is a catalyst for changing lives…and not just those of its grant recipients.

The bowling pin is a visual reminder to me of Peter's fingerprint on our organization. And, every time the chips are down, I reach over and touch my left shoulder – a symbolic gesture that reminds me of my love for my brother and a reminder from him that "the right thing will happen—just keep doing the right things."

Almost one hundred of our 126 members attended the first Annual Meeting. We celebrated over dinner and then each of the nonprofit finalists gave a ten-minute presentation about their proposed program as women listened attentively and voted accordingly. After mingling for twenty minutes, we called our members back together to announce the winner.

LifeWorks received our first grant. The chair of the grant review committee that had recommended LifeWorks as a finalist called Susan, the Executive Director, about two hours before the meeting started. Offhandedly, she asked Susan what she was planning to wear.

Susan excitedly replied, "I've done a lot of thinking about that, and I have on my dark power pin-striped pant suit with a white blouse. It says 'I mean business', and I feel really good."

Without missing a beat, the chair responded, "Stop what you are doing and meet me at Ann Taylor as soon as you can. We need to soften you up!"

Before Susan knew it, she owned a beautiful black top with a soft neckline and a pair of tailored white pants—making a mess of the fitting room in the process by ripping off tags as she donned her new outfit—only to hurriedly stuff her pin-striped suit in the shopping bag as she dashed off to the meeting. She stepped out of her car looking serious, but approachable, and it worked. She kiddingly says that not only did she receive the first Impact Austin grant, but she also got the fastest (and only!) Impact Austin makeover in our history. We have laughed about this with Susan, and she tells us lovingly that we are different than other funders… in the best way.

As our members left that first Annual Meeting, their observations convinced me that Impact Austin was not going to be a one-trick pony and quickly disappear.

I heard women say things like, "Each finalist proposed a compelling project, which made voting hard."

"There is so much need in this community; we have to get 200 members next year so we can give two grants."

"Even though my first choice didn't get the grant, I'm satisfied with the outcome of the vote."

These comments and others like them solidified our board's thinking. We set a new goal of growing our membership by one hundred women a year so that in our fifth year we could give a $100,000 grant in each of our five focus areas. We knew we could do it by asking our members to invite women in their networks to join. When we saw women expand their power in giving back by encouraging their friends to invest, we recognized we had a winning formula.

5

ROLE MODELING

*"Here's to naïve optimism and always
believing we can change the world.
Here's to a lifetime friendship forged in the fire
of creating things together that really matter.
Here's to our sisterhood born of hard truths,
profound respect, deep affection and sheer persistence."*

—Glenda Holmstrom

In the process of growing Impact Austin, I grew personally. Though, sometimes in very painful ways.

During the first year, as recruiting heated up, life turned more crazy. Two or three nights a week, I shared the Impact Austin story in women's homes with the intention of getting their friends to join our organization. I left home at about 6:15 p.m. and returned around 9:30 p.m. most nights.

The hostesses usually put out a wonderful spread with food and wine, and I promised myself that I would only have a glass of water at these "coffees." I knew I'd gain unneeded weight if I didn't curb my enthusiasm at the snack table, and I kept that "no eating" promise to myself as I spoke at hundreds of coffees over the years. That's not to say that during the day I didn't spend a lot of time in drive-thru lanes at fast food restaurants.

Initially, I justified the fast food option because I ate and drove at the same time, making it possible to squeeze in one more appointment. Thankfully, I never had an accident, but my car looked like a war zone inside. I hid the evidence from my husband and kids by stuffing my trash in the outside garbage can way down at the bottom so they wouldn't know. Not that anyone was looking for it—it was my guilt over the cost in term of dollars and calories—both unnecessary—that brought me to my senses. As a result of that temporary madness, I challenged myself to spend less than $10 a week on food and snacks outside of the house. That $10 bought three skim lattes at a local coffee shop that I used for meetings.

It made the baloney-sandwich-with-mustard option for lunch at home a common occurrence. I truly get excited about that combo, especially when the bread is so fresh that it sticks to the roof of my mouth. Besides, baloney is cheap, satisfying and doesn't come with killer fries that I cannot resist. Plus, I can eat the sandwich while checking my emails. I am prone to multi-tasking and sometimes take it to a level that scares even me. I can do laundry, answer email, eat lunch and watch a television show all at the same time. I'm not saying I do my best work when I am that busy, but it's a way to get everything done in a day.

Since those I worked with were volunteers, I wanted to be as flexible as possible with them. Some could meet early in the morning, some for lunch, some only in the evening. That's what made life crazy at our house. My family couldn't keep up with my schedule, and it changed often. With teenagers who played school sports, our schedule was crazy already. But, for the first time, I was the one missing games because of my evening commitments. Phil was the anchor and made sure at least one of us attended the sporting events.

It bothered me a lot at first, and then like that frog you put in warm water and keep adding hotter and hotter water—I didn't notice the pace of my life getting out of control. After a coffee, I sent thank you emails to the women who joined that evening, answered emails, did some paperwork and then sat in front of the tv to unwind before going to bed. Normally, less than six hours later, it started all over again. Day-after-day turned into month-after-month and then year-after-year.

One evening, Phil sat me down and asked me to confront reality. It was not a pleasant conversation and ended with me pouting and him exhausted.

"Reb, I know you love what you are doing, and I want to support you. I just want to make sure that your priorities are aligned with our family's, and I'm still looking for balance here just like the last time we had this conversation."

My incredulous response surprised me, "I've found something that really excites me, and I can make a difference at the same time. What's wrong with that? You had your chapter, and now it's my turn to fly."

We went back and forth until there was nothing left to say and no resolution in sight. I was single-minded about Impact Austin and *loved* every minute I spent working on this fledgling. It was fun, exciting, scary and full of learning opportunities for me. It energized me in a way I had *never* experienced. My confidence soared. Talking to anybody about what I was doing made my heart smile: a prospective member, a potential investor to help us with operating funds, the media as they tried to get a handle on what collective giving was. With each successive conversation, my conviction grew—getting me ready to take on the next challenge. Sharing the Impact Austin story came naturally and women listened.

Since speaking opportunities usually happened in the evening, they took me away from Phil and the kids. As young teenagers, they weren't sad that I was gone until they had a spontaneous life issue to discuss that only moms can understand.

One day Claire came to me and said, "Mom, I know you love what you are doing. I just wish sometimes I could sit on the floor in your office and chat while you are working. Even if it's about nothing. It's just that when I want to do it, you are not here."

Brad's approach differed but stung no less. "I don't even ask if you are coming to one of my games anymore because the answer will be 'no' and the reason will be Impact Austin."

My family's disappointment started to sink in, and I headed for the deck with a cup of coffee one morning to see what wisdom the barn swallow had for me. He was already there waiting and had a lot to say. "This is getting serious, and you've got to get a hold of yourself. You are trusting the devil's cape right now, and it's full of ego and lies and grandiosity. Is that what you really want?"

Sarcastically, I answered, "Oh, so you have issues with me, too. Nice."

The longer I sat there and the colder my coffee got, the more I let down my defenses and started thinking about what Brad, Claire and Phil had said. Wow, I'd been totally unavailable to my family. Even when I was with them, it was only physically. My mind was constantly with Impact Austin. While I'd thanked Phil often for being the anchor for our family the last few years, he'd grown tired of that role (that he had never asked for in the first place) and desired the freedom and flexibility he sought in early retirement. I'd been incorrectly thinking all along that because I was "doing good" it was all okay. And that if my family didn't understand that, they were just being slow on the uptake and not being very supportive of me.

"Now you're getting somewhere," affirmed the swallow, "You have finally acknowledged that your ego has been controlling your actions and your words. That's progress. Go apologize to Phil for some of your impolite comments, and you better go hug your kids for no reason. You being immersed in "doing good" should not make life harder on those you love most. Now, get busy and make amends."

As I went back inside, I realized that Phil and I had both given sacrificially to Impact Austin. While it wasn't always smooth sailing, we weathered each storm the best we could. Another one of my musings reveals my struggling heart at the time.

Tomorrow, please come quickly.

Have you ever felt like, no matter what you do or say, it's not the right action or the right answer? Today started out beautifully with the sun shining in my eyes and possibilities teeming in its rays. However, the day is ending with a shroud of darkness I didn't anticipate. I'm glad I didn't know to expect it, or I would not have appreciated the part of my day that was filled with compassion, hope and belief in the human spirit. However, the darkness just hit me in the face like a 2X4. Now, I begin to think of other moments of darkness I've had in the past week, and I feel overwhelmed. There is a reason for all of this, but my heart hurts right now, and I'm not sure what to make of it.

What is the lesson I'm supposed to learn? How can I grow from this? Whose life can be better because I've grown? I am weary. I am going to put my head on my pillow. I will thank God for bringing me through this day. I will ask for His will to be done. I will be patient for once. And, I will listen. Tomorrow will bring new experiences, new ideas, new possibilities. I will always be thankful for the half-full glass that accompanied my birth. It serves me well at times like this. A tonic. A blessing. A godsend.

Phil helped serve wine at the social hour preceding our fifth Annual Meeting in June, 2008. He had no idea what to expect and smiled when he realized hundreds of women had gathered to vote for that year's grant recipients. When the social hour ended and he was leaving, he gave me a kiss and whispered "good luck." When I returned home that evening, his appreciation for Impact Austin had changed. That epiphany ushered in a fondness for and an interest in my work that had not existed previously.

As I look back over the life of Impact Austin, I am so grateful for Phil's quiet fortitude; his support from the sidelines, which has been more important than being on the front line. He has given money in meaningful amounts and helped me sort through my emotions in difficult situations with members. He edited my letters and had a keen sense of how to share a message in a compelling way. He ordered pizza and cooked dinner often when I was burning the candle at both ends.

He has a servant's attitude, and he never draws attention to himself. I never knew Phil talked to anyone about what I do, but I found out from his sister just how proud of me he is. He doesn't express that to me directly, but I know he is happy for my success. That means the world to me.

Brad was almost sixteen when Peter died. He was a high school sophomore with a very active social calendar, lots of friends and a strong personality. He was a good baseball player, and as parents, we were glad that practices and off-season weight room conditioning took most of his time during the school year. Brad lived on the edge in all areas of his life, and I believe he came out of the womb with that approach to life in mind. He held to his convictions, even if it made life more difficult for him.

He came home from school one day telling me he would not get a good mid-term grade in Pre-Calculus. I had learned not to get excited when he made statements like this, so I just said, "Oh, really? Why?"

He explained that he was supposed to turn in homework each day, and that he had not done so, which meant his homework grade was a zero. I asked what his response to the teacher was when he had nothing to show. Brad's reply was so, well...Brad.

"I told him that the homework we were doing was a review of the Algebra II class I took last year. I got an A in that class and remember the concepts. I signed up for Pre-Calculus this year, and when we start learning Pre-Calculus, I'll do my homework."

While Brad's approach needed polish and politeness, I admired his ability to stick to his convictions. The teacher was not impressed, and they had a few battles throughout the year. But, Brad got an A in the class and felt some satisfaction in making his point. He tells me he's a lot like me…hmmmm.

Brad was sad for me that my brother died, but he didn't know Peter that well; so his sense of loss was not as acute as mine. He loved Peter's two young adult kids and looked forward to keeping that connection tight. Just like his sister, Brad had seen a change in me as I worked to get Impact Austin off the ground. Prior to this, I was his mom who did his laundry, cooked his meals (many of which did not meet his standards) and shuttled him around town for various social and school activities.

I had resigned myself to the fact that I was a wallet and car keys for both of my children. Though, some of my best conversations with my young teenage kids happened as I was taking them to and from activities—especially if they were in the back seat. There was something very safe in their minds about talking to the back of Mom's head—a totally different experience than being next to me in the front seat. No eye contact. No obvious judgment from me. I didn't realize how special that time was until they both got their licenses and could do the driving themselves. I still miss those conversations from the backseat and all of the listening I did as I ferried their friends around, too.

As soon as Brad got his driver's license, he started working on the grill line at Fuddrucker's. He learned a whole new Spanish vocabulary there and enjoyed the challenge of conversing with his co-workers while they took great pleasure in being his teachers. He coupled that with his classroom Spanish and declared himself fluent.

Brad secretly announced to Phil and Claire that he planned to give me $100 for Christmas that year. Now that he was working, he wanted to write a check to Impact Austin to help support my efforts. When Brad announced on Christmas Day that his present to me was hiding within the branches of the Christmas tree, my heart soared. That's where we put gift checks from relatives; so I was hoping his was a gift to Impact Austin. And sure enough, Brad had done just what he promised and absolutely beamed as I smothered him in kisses and hugs. It was the first time I witnessed my son being philanthropic, and that humbled me.

The day kept getting better....

I had been busy during the weeks building up to Christmas trying to find the last few members that would get us to our membership goal. I had noticed, in passing, that the kitchen pantry and a few closets looked neater than usual, assumed Phil was the culprit and didn't give it a second thought. I was grateful for his help, but it didn't seem like a big deal. Pantries and closets get messy sometimes. Smug, I know.

On Christmas morning, I learned that Claire had done the cleaning. She observed my work with Impact Austin over the previous nine months and saw the joy I got from building the organization and getting women to join together to make a difference in the community. She wanted to show her support by giving $100 to Impact Austin, too. At thirteen years of age, she did not have $100 to give and asked her father for help. He encouraged her to earn it by doing chores around the house.

She had a few dollars in babysitting money saved up in her drawer and knew exactly how much more she needed to meet her goal. Phil and Claire laid out a plan, which included cleaning out the pantry and closets. By a few days before Christmas, she had saved up $97. She asked Phil's permission to go thru his drawers and car console to find and claim any loose change. He agreed, and that treasure hunt paid off.

We had had a great time as a family watching each other open our gifts that Christmas morning. We laughed a lot and everyone was pleased with what Santa brought. I thought the gift-giving portion of the day had ended and busied myself with putting discarded ribbons and paper in oversized trash bags as Claire approached me with the most beautiful smile on her face and a crumpled envelope in her hands that she was cradling with much care.

"Mom, I've never seen you so happy, and I want to make a difference, too. So, here's $100 to help Impact Austin buy paper clips." As she beamed with pride about her accomplishment, she handed me the little envelope which contained mostly $5 and $1 bills with $3 in loose change weighing down the bottom. She brought me to tears when she said, "I want to be a member of Impact Austin when I grow up, too."

"Oh, Sweetie! I'm trying to hold back these happy tears, but I don't think I can. I am so grateful for your gift and that you earned every penny. I'm even more excited that you want to give back, too."

I hugged her to my chest as my heart exploded with gratitude and the realization that I had been role modeling the joy that comes from giving back in spite of the angst I had caused my family. While Claire and I shared tears of joy, the boys didn't cry, but I knew they were moved because they couldn't talk for fear of crying. The moment was beautiful in its simplicity and poignant beyond words.

When our emotions had settled down a bit, I looked at Claire and suggested, "Sweetie, you don't have to wait to join Impact Austin as an adult. Why don't you get your girlfriends and their friends to give $100, pool the money, and give a grant to a non-profit that supports something meaningful to you like underserved youth?"

"Wow, that's something to think about, Mom." At least she liked the idea, and we left it at that.

Our short exchange reminded me of my experience with Junior Achievement when I was a junior in high school. It was new to our small farm town and gave me something to learn outside of the classroom. I convinced a few of my close high school girlfriends to join with me because we knew how to have fun in any situation, especially when it included a chance to flirt with boys.

In those days, each JA chapter started and ran a manufacturing business during the school year. We met weekly and had to make lots of start-up decisions like our company name, the role for each worker, the product we would manufacture and the price we'd sell it for. We chose to make bacon de-curlers—round metal disks with holes in them with a heat resistant knob attached in the middle.

Our advisors, local young Caterpillar Tractor Company executives, helped us run the business. I took on the treasurer role, which really meant I was the bookkeeper. I had no idea what I was getting into, but it sounded like fun, and I was good at math. So, how hard could it be? It challenged me more than I admitted to anyone. By default, I learned about profit and loss, breakeven, and cost of goods sold. While I won an award for doing my job well, I learned that working with numbers didn't excite me. However, sales did!

We each had to sell our product, and I took that role very seriously, rehearsing my sales pitch in my bedroom mirror until I could say it with confidence. Then I practiced on my younger brother and sister who sat on my bed and made faces as I gave them my sales pitch, daring me to lose my concentration and stumble over my words. It was a game to them, and I accepted the challenge.

After much practice, I made my first real sales call on my parents in the den. While I knew they would buy my product, I wanted to legitimately earn their business and also let them see how seriously I took my job.

Armed with confidence from the successful sale of my first bacon de-curler, I started going up and down the street making sales calls, and one by one my neighbors bought the $1 contraption. My biggest sale came from a neighbor who bought seven because he had multiple family members in town who loved bacon. He secretly told my parents that my enthusiasm for my product was contagious, and he just had to buy more than one.

I look back now and realize that experience set the stage for all of the selling I've done in my life. Years later as a young IBM sales rep, I became a Junior Achievement advisor because I knew what that experience taught me, and I wanted to give that opportunity to other teenagers.

That reminiscing brought me back to the present, thinking about my teenagers. Both kids stretched that year. Claire, because she had no real means of income and was determined to give Impact Austin $100. Brad, because he normally focused on himself 24/7, and this was truly a beautiful departure from the norm. To top it all off, Phil acted as the linchpin again—keeping them both focused and helping them understand the huge significance of their gifts and what it meant to Impact Austin, me and our family. In the end, words don't matter. Actions do.

Since Impact Austin had not been through its first grant application and review process yet, it didn't make sense to act immediately on the idea Claire and I had discussed. By 2005, a young member named Lisa joined our board, and she was the perfect candidate for leading this effort to teach the art and importance of giving to the next generation of young women.

Over the ensuing months, she created a sound framework for the organization, using the Impact Austin model as a guide, and then started recruiting girls. She was young and had no children. Somehow, that made her smarter and easier to relate to for the eighth- through twelfth-grade girls we wanted to attract.

Claire loved being part of the founding group of girls who named themselves Girls Giving Grants (G3). However, she made a serious request, "Mom, I want this to be something I do on my own. I don't want you looking over my shoulder or anyone else's and second-guessing decisions we might make as a group. I like that someone who is not a mom is going to help us get started. Will you make sure that other moms are not allowed to hover over their daughters as we put this thing together?"

I was taken aback at first, but then I realized the maturity of her request. She didn't know what lay ahead, but she was confident they could, with Lisa's guidance, create an organization and a process that worked. She wanted the members of this girls' group to take pride in and ownership of the decisions they made—because they followed a reasoned process, not because their moms told them what to do. As hard as it was to let go, I decided to trust Claire's instincts. That decision paid off in spades.

Claire, who had recently earned $100 to give me for Christmas, asked her father if he'd give her the $100 she needed to join G3. Phil quickly responded, "Claire, if you earn this $100 also, you'll invest more fully in the research of the organizations that apply for the G3 grant, and you'll take more pride in the final decision."

Initially, Claire wasn't happy, but in the end, she was proud to say she had earned the $100 she gave to G3. That first year, twenty-one girls gave a total of $2,100. They were so proud of what they had contributed and could hardly wait to get started.

As the girls got closer to the final vote to decide which nonprofit organization would get the grant, Claire asked me an insightful question. "Mom, one of our finalists will use our money to impact (her word!) a lot of kids, but not very deeply. The other finalist will use our money to impact a few kids, but more deeply. Which is the bigger impact?"

At the time she asked the question, I was driving sixty-five miles per hour down a highway bringing her home from her G3 meeting. I was stunned by the depth of her understanding of how one might measure impact and wanted to reach over and hug her.

I wanted to tell her that one of the beautiful benefits of starting Impact Austin was seeing my young teenage daughter grow in her understanding of what it means to make an impact.

Instead, deciding to keep my cool, I responded by saying, "That's a question we wrestle with all the time in our grant review meetings. You will have to make your decision based on all that you know and trust that others will do the same." She smiled at me, and I could tell she was glad I didn't give her a lecture. I was pleased that I didn't do that either.

In 2006, the girls gave their first grant to the Austin Children's Shelter, and Claire decided immediately afterwards to go volunteer for them. She had to take some mandatory classes, and it was not easy to get certified to be a volunteer there. She wanted to play with the children, and that meant she had to pass a background check and successfully complete the training. Again, my heart swelled because I knew Claire's impetus for wanting to volunteer came as a natural result of her learning about the needs of these kids.

She continued to volunteer at The George Washington University (GW) while a student there. In fact, she titled her college essay "From Death to Philanthropy" and wrote about her personal journey to becoming a philanthropist as a result of the death of her uncle and seeing the change in her mom. I had no idea until she asked me to fact-check the content of her essay. I couldn't get past the first paragraph without crying. It revealed her true feelings about the impact I had had on her as a mom and a budding philanthropist. I keep a copy of the essay in my toast rack on my desk and read it occasionally. It feels like a warm hug from Claire, and I never get tired of it.

While a junior in college, Claire started a chapter of Engineers Without Borders (EWB) and got her fellow engineering classmates to join in the effort. They had to raise a certain amount of money before being assigned their first project: building outdoor latrines for families in a rural mountain village in El Salvador. To say it was life-changing for her is an understatement. Claire continued to visit the village on her own after college because she wanted to finish what her EWB college chapter had started. In the process, she fell in love with a young man in that village. Julio and Claire got married in the tiny church there in March, 2017, and lived apart until he moved to the US later that year. They got married again in the US in 2018 with many friends and family celebrating this special union. Claire's journey continually reminds me that philanthropy is learned and starting early pays dividends.

G3 is unique to Impact Austin; one of our members, Dina, ran the program single-handedly as a volunteer for nine years after its initial start-up phase. She was a young, single professional and had been involved in philanthropy in her sorority in college. She had also learned a lot about leadership and wanted to give the G3 girls an opportunity to experience both. By the time she retired from this role, hundreds of girls had graduated from the program, and many credited her with igniting their passion to give back.

Dina excelled at advising and giving the G3 members the responsibility of leading and running the program. She derived great pleasure from mentoring and encouraging them to invest fully in the experience. For those that did, she wrote many college recommendation letters. She also set healthy boundaries with the girls' parents.

In one instance, a mom called Dina to complain that her daughter had not been selected for a certain leadership role the following year. Dina politely told the mom that she'd be happy to have a conversation with her daughter, if the daughter contacted her directly. Adults got the message loud and clear that G3 provided leadership development opportunities for the girls, and they didn't need their parents intervening on their behalf.

Her enthusiasm for developing young leaders through the G3 program rubbed off on the girls, too. Several majored in nonprofit studies in college, and a few have returned as advisors to the program in recent years because they know firsthand how powerful the experience was. While Dina no longer leads G3, she has forged lasting relationships with former participants. She also has three young daughters and is already looking forward to when they will join G3. She is a powerful woman raising powerful young women.

6

LEARNING AS I GROW

"Have you learned lessons only of those who admired you, and were tender with you, and stood aside for you? Have you not learned the great lessons of those who rejected you, and braced themselves against you? Or who treated you with contempt, or disputed passage with you? Have you had no practice to receive opponents when they come?"

—Walt Whitman

Impact Austin encountered predictable challenges and surprising successes during my leadership tenure, and I attribute both to the people, places and things that made this journey life-changing for me. Certain inflection points required serious pivots in my behavior and attitudes. I learned from every interaction, and by sharing some of these vivid memories, I am reminded that we all have the power to change our circumstances.

*   *   *

Some people are catalysts for change. I met Brett in 2005, and he's that person. Though, I didn't realize it at first or in the way you might think. Brett attended a brief meeting in my home for the grant finalists so they could learn more about the process of preparing their presentations to our members at the upcoming Annual Meeting.

The assembled group included a representative from each of the five finalist organizations and the five Impact Austin members who had chaired the corresponding grant review committees. Naturally, there was nervous tension in the air because two of the organizations were each going to receive a $100,500 grant from Impact Austin in just a few weeks.

The meeting started with the finalists introducing themselves and stating their roles in their organizations. That went smoothly until Brett raised his hand and asked, "Would it be okay for each finalist to share what program or project they are proposing—just to give everyone some context?"

I politely, but firmly, denied his request because I wanted to keep the agenda moving. What I didn't notice was the mortified look on his face and his sense that he'd ruined his organization's chances due to his seemingly inappropriate question. I learned of this afterwards from his Impact Austin committee chair and dismissed the issue.

A few months later, I entered a yearlong leadership class that included an opening retreat. As I approached the registration table, I saw Brett's nametag and did a double-take just as he came up. We both said a polite "hello, it's great to see you" that made us each uncomfortable. We agreed that it would be nice to get to know each other over the coming year, but I'm sure neither of us meant what we said.

One of our assignments required us to have a Walk and Talk with each of the other fifty three classmates over the course of that year. Brett reached out to me several weeks into the program, and we met for coffee on a Sunday afternoon. I only went out of obligation because I didn't relish the possibility of revisiting his experience at the luncheon. We started with the usual pleasantries, and then things got real. He shared that he had lost his sister to cancer just like I had lost Peter. That revelation changed *everything* for both of us.

Instead of talking about our professional backgrounds and why we joined the leadership class, we talked about our siblings, sharing our feelings about loss and how it impacted us. That led to us feeling like we could be more vulnerable and authentic with each other as the conversation continued. What started as an obligatory conversation ended with each of us feeling we had made a new friend on a level deeper than we had expected. He was the bigger person—reaching out to me in spite of our inauspicious start back in May. I vividly remember driving home from that meeting with a smile on my face and a heart full of gratitude.

Our friendship deepened over the years. He knows our family well and even officiated our daughter's wedding in 2018. Our birthdays are one day apart, and we celebrate them together—usually over a happy hour glass of wine at a local restaurant. Who knew an annoying first encounter would turn into a beautiful partnership? I count our friendship as one of the best gifts I have received as a result of Peter's death. Brett changed my heart just by being himself, and his sense of humor reminds me of my brother's. That's worth cherishing. Thanks, Brett.

*   *   *

On Mother's Day, 2006, Phil gave me a beautiful bracelet with a charm I designed that serves as a constant connection to my brother. While Peter figuratively sits on my left shoulder, I wanted something physical to symbolize his presence. The two-sided charm boasts a reproduction of the Impact Austin logo on the front and our tagline on the back with the date we extended our first grant. "Ordinary Women...Extraordinary Impact 6-12-04." The designer worked patiently with me and did not quit until she knew the design was right. She gave me the mold so that no one else could copy it, which makes it even more special to me. Over time, the charm has accumulated small dents and scratches. It reminds me of my relationship with Peter. There were lots of scratches and dents in our relationship over the years, but nothing that marred the overall beauty of what we celebrated in each other.

On a few special occasions, additional charms joined the flower. A bowling pin, Peter's birthstone and a high heeled shoe representing Impact Austin members. There's still room for a book and a cape. Both of those will complete the bracelet.

*   *   *

Impact Austin experienced some early success, and we had a lot to share about our giving model. Thanks to a member with great media connections, CBS took an interest—so much so that one of its field teams travelled to Austin in 2006 to film a segment for the CBS Evening News with Katie Couric. It was scheduled for Monday during the week of Thanksgiving as CBS highlighted "Giving in America." Phil and I settled onto the sofa, each with our own fluffy throws covering us, as we waited for the story to air. Just as Katie Couric announced the Impact Austin piece, only video displayed—no audio. Phil and I looked at each other incredulously. In that single moment, I learned a lesson in humility.

My phone started ringing off the hook and my email inbox blew up because we told everyone we knew to watch the CBS Evening News that night. In a moment of clarity, I realized I had the opportunity to *lead* with my response to our disgruntled members and calmly responded to four different callers saying, "I know you are disappointed. I am too. However, the fact that we didn't make the national news will not change how we recruit new members or how we deliver on our mission. And, I am choosing to believe the segment didn't run tonight because someone who is not home right now was supposed to see this."

Katie Couric signed off saying, "We will bring you this story tomorrow night."

We hadn't missed our chance after all. Our members and friends reassembled in front of their TVs on Tuesday and enjoyed the story about Impact Austin. And sure enough, a woman in St. Louis saw the Tuesday feed and started a group like ours in her community. Life unfolds as it should, and I celebrate times like this with Peter, who reminds me it all works out—just not in the way we think it will sometimes.

*   *   *

Even in the toughest times for Impact Austin, there wasn't a moment I felt like I couldn't go on. However, in October, 2007, my mettle was tested when our family was suddenly rocked to its core. Brad made outstanding grades at his challenging college prep high school. He joined a great fraternity at TCU and had many friends...both guys and girls. He convinced us that getting his own apartment after his sophomore year was a great idea, and we agreed. He had an intern job that paid him well and could support him financially to the extent we weren't willing.

Phil had an inkling something wasn't right in Ft. Worth, as only a parent can, and decided to change some travel plans to pop in on Brad. His gut was right, and what he discovered was difficult for a parent to face. For all of the success Brad had experienced in high school, college presented some challenges he didn't have the tools to navigate. While the story ends well, the journey to get there was not easy. There was no dress rehearsal for this. We had to rely on the advice of others and find those we trusted and respected. We had little time to react, and our decision could be the best or worst of our lives. Brad withdrew from TCU in order to take a "time out" and deal with his issues.

I didn't share facts indiscriminately, but I didn't hide them either. It was important to me not to keep secrets. It helped me cope and continue to advance Impact Austin. One of the things I learned as a result of this experience is that there is no family free from life's issues. We all have times of stress, tragedy, disappointment and failure. In my mind, I had always seen our family holding hands as we skipped across the high school football field into the sunset. Kids who got good grades, would go to college and get good jobs—all without a hiccup. While I learned that was sheer fantasy, I was about to learn more about myself.

My family, friends and Impact Austin colleagues have made comments over the last several years about the positive change they've seen in me and how I interact with them. While I fail miserably at times and fall back into bad behaviors, I recognize when I'm behaving badly and work to correct it. Brad's life challenges gave me a chance to examine myself and change course.

Brad subsequently re-enrolled at TCU and graduated in May, 2010. He returned to the scene of the crime armed with new life skills and navigated the last three semesters beautifully. His academic advisor told him that one of his professors had noticed a **huge** change in his attitude and willingness to work hard and be a positive class participant. Brad called to tell me this while I was driving, and I remember pulling over to wipe the joyful tears from my eyes. He had learned redemption— that one can come back from the brink of destruction and succeed. He didn't use that word, but he was so proud of himself and so thankful that a professor he had treated poorly in the past saw the change in him and had taken the time to tell someone. The only thing that would have been better for me is if I could have seen the smile on his face as he shared his joy. It's a phone call I'll never forget.

Over the years, I have learned that my most important job is just to love my son—unconditionally and without judgment. We've also learned how to set boundaries for our relationship so that we both know what constitutes "crossing the line" and call each other on it in very calm terms. And finally, I have released my son. I cannot fix or control him, but I can **love** him. I cannot ease the consequences of his actions and choices, but I can always love him through the pain. Fortunately, this change in our relationship has given way to lots of celebration for his successes—big and small. If he's excited, I am too. Before, I'd easily find something that he didn't do quite right or something he could have done better. Now, no judgment—just love. I'm still in awe of all that I've learned and how much stronger our family is as a result.

Brad's issues highlighted my shortcomings. My desire to make things better, if for no other reason than to relieve tension in the house and in my heart. It gave me the chance to learn the meaning and beauty of boundaries. We can now be together in the same place, but we each have our space and we honor the other's right to a different opinion—not just when we're in a good mood, but all of the time. There's respect and affection. When he comes home for brief visits, he walks in the front door, drops all that he is carrying and gives me a warm hug that is never long enough.

This reminds me of the nonjudgmental love Peter and I had for each other. We held different beliefs politically, religiously and even with regard to child-rearing. We lived very different lives as adults and became strangers for a while. As soon as he shared his diagnosis with me in December, 2002, a different kind of love took over. I remember feeling only unconditional love for my brother as we were Instant Messaging those last few weeks. Honoring his thoughts, listening to his heart as he "talked" about his kids and how proud he was of them. Understanding his need to dump some baggage. Promising to be a sounding board for whatever he needed to say and feel. I remember feeling privileged that my brother opened up to me with unmitigated honesty, and I'm reliving my loving relationship with him as Brad and I, who were like strangers not so long ago, begin to share ourselves with each other honestly. It brings indescribable joy and a few happy tears as we find our own special way to love each other.

In 2009, *Austin Woman* selected me to appear on the cover of their magazine with a multi-page story inside, and Brad asked me for a copy. His interest surprised me and I said, "Buddy, I'm thrilled you want to read the article and learn more about Impact Austin."

I laughed hysterically at his response. "Oh, no, Mom. I don't want to read the article. I want to put the magazine on the front passenger seat of my car so that when I have a hot date with a cool girl, she'll have to move the magazine when she gets in. I'll get to tell her the woman on the cover is my mother. And somehow that will make me cool, too." Brad is still single all these years later. You can draw your own conclusion about the effectiveness of his strategy.

Buddy—my son, my friend

*How do you describe the unique relationship between a mother and her son? Buddy, as I am fond of calling him, can be totally charming and equally exasperating when he gets under my skin. He and I have sparred for twenty three years now. I think the score is pretty close to even, but I'm not really keeping track, except to record the fact that our love for each other **never** wanes. Our **like** for each other is another story depending on our moods. We are mirror images, and that can be disastrous, especially when one of us is feeling inadequate, nervous or anxious. We wear our feelings on our sleeves and pay the consequences accordingly. Buddy has taught me to laugh at life's absurdities and to love country music. He knows how to have fun, and he dares me to join in. He has street smarts out the wazoo and is always thinking ahead. On more than one occasion, he has given me advice about the care and feeding of Impact Austin. He sees* *possibilities. He dreams big. He doesn't let "no" get in his way. Yes, we are mirror images, and I'm grateful.*

*   *   *

As Impact Austin grew, the daily needs of the business expanded too. I still held things together and made sure everything got done, but I was reaching my maximum capacity with no apparent relief in sight. That all changed when Kathrine showed up just in time to bail me out, though she didn't know that was her purpose initially.

We met at a recruiting event, and she immediately wanted to know what volunteer opportunities existed and how she might engage. Her quiet confidence, business background and list of detail-oriented questions confirmed for me that she could provide the support I needed.

Soon, we finalized the Executive Administrator position at my kitchen table, and she got busy. I relied on her to figure things out on her own because I didn't have the time to babysit or cajole. She didn't need direction and continually over-delivered. At times, she bossed me around—that's when I knew she was a **perfect** fit.

While all of that made Impact Austin better and made my workload more manageable, Kathrine's loyalty set her apart from other volunteers. She cared deeply about the organization and even more about me. She never betrayed my confidence and always had my back. Kathrine also taught me that philanthropy is a connection between the head and the heart. It has little to do with the pocketbook.

Impact Austin regularly attracted the right women with the necessary skills who were looking for meaningful volunteer engagement. Where did these women come from and how did they know they had the skills we needed? What was it about our culture that intrigued them? I don't have the answers. I attribute it to the fact that a force larger than any one of us guides this journey. I call that force God. Others may call it something else.

*   *   *

Our constant, steady growth over the first five years gave me the courage to dream big. Early in 2008, I read *The Soul of Money*, written by Lynne Twist. Her message about abundance vs. scarcity transformed my relationship with money and set me on a path of increasing my philanthropy in a way I never thought possible.

Instinctively, I knew Lynne Twist had to speak to our members and inspire them on their philanthropic journeys just as she had done for me. With conviction and a little bit of fear, I picked up the phone and called Lynne's organization to find out just how far out of reach her speaking fee was. Her assistant told me $12,000 plus travel expenses, and I sensed she expected me to say we could not afford it. Instead, I asked what Lynne's availability was in October as if the fee was not a problem at all. When, in reality, I had **no** idea how Impact Austin could afford her.

I learned that paying a 10% deposit would lock in the date, and it took me less than 2 seconds to respond, "Where do I send the $1200? We look forward to Lynne inspiring our members in October."

My brain swirled with fundraising ideas. I knew I could find $1200 for the deposit. The remaining $10,800 was a problem. Once again, I had taken a leap of faith and trusted my cape.

At the time, one of our members was managing director with a woman-owned wealth management firm. She invited me to have lunch with their founder and the Austin executive team. I was thrilled to share the Impact Austin story with them, hoping to get a few to invest as members. I got so much more!

At that meeting, I also talked about Lynne Twist's upcoming presentation in October and how inspiring our members to increase their personal philanthropy was something Impact Austin deemed important. The founder spontaneously asked what Lynne's speaker fee was and agreed to underwrite the whole amount. I was overwhelmed with gratitude and relief—my cape had not failed me! The firm underwrote our Speaker Series for the following two years because the founder believed in the power of women to change the world. She passed away in 2019, leaving a legacy of impactful philanthropy that had included Impact Austin.

Lynne Twist landed in Austin with just a few hours to spare before speaking to our members. Her original flight from San Francisco had been cancelled due to fog, and she scrambled to make last minute changes in order to arrive in Austin on time. When I approached the airport to pick her up, she texted me to say she was in a bathroom stall in baggage claim changing into her speaking clothes and asked me to keep circling until she texted me from curbside pick-up. That alone let me know that she was down to earth and authentic—my kind of woman. When she got in my car, she didn't complain about her difficult travel day or changing clothes in a bathroom stall.

Before she had even settled into the passenger seat, she started asking questions. "Now, tell me more about Impact Austin and its members. Who are these women and why did you start this organization?"

I answered those questions quickly and easily and then she said, "Thank you for reading my book. Was there something particularly inspiring that you read?"

Excitedly, I replied, "The two sentences above the first paragraph in Chapter 4. 'When you let go of trying to get more of what you don't really need, it frees up oceans of energy to make a difference with what you have. When you make a difference with what you have, it expands.' As you can see, I've memorized those words because they fundamentally changed my relationship with money."

"Oh, Rebecca. You have made my day. When people understand that, the universe opens up in the most beautiful way. Thank you for sharing. And, I must say I'm impressed that you know the sentences by heart!"

We arrived at the speaking venue with just minutes to spare, and she didn't skip a beat. Her message resonated powerfully with our members, many of whom still credit her with positively changing their philosophy about money. She stayed well into the evening to sign books for every attendee and relished in the opportunity she'd been given to touch hearts.

Lynne also agreed to stay with one of our founding board members so that we could reduce the cost of her travel expenses. I had asked Nancy if she'd be willing to host Lynne for the night because Nancy exudes warmth and enjoys having guests. Little did I know that by 8am the next morning Nancy would become a significant donor to the Nobel Women's Initiative that Lynne was a part of. They have become fast friends, and other Impact Austin women have also invested in that initiative. Again, I was reminded that our impact is so much more than the grants we give in the community. It's something I never dreamed of when I was just trying to heal the hole in my heart.

If you never ask, you'll never know.

I've never met him in person. One phone call, several emails and a few Facebook interactions account for our relationship. His name is Kevin Salwen, and he wrote The Power of Half with his teenage daughter. It's a powerfully written account of one family's unorthodox philanthropic experience and how it changed their lives.

A friend of mine sat next to Kevin during a break at a conference last February in San Diego. They talked; she was enamored. She emailed me soon after and mentioned her conversation with Kevin, whom she thought was a lovely man with a compelling story. Immediately, I went to work. With all the bravado I could muster, I sent him an email introducing him to Impact Austin, asking if he would be willing to come speak to us in October for a fee we could afford.

"I know this is a stab in the dark, but all you can say is 'no'. Though, I'm hoping you'll surprise us and say 'yes'!"

Having no idea if he checked his email very often or if he had 'handlers' that ran interference, I figured I'd be lucky to get a response. But, at least I had asked the question. Gratitude (and complete shock!) filled my heart when Kevin replied less than four hours later saying he liked the idea of women pooling their financial resources; he'd love to speak and that October was wide open. Indeed, he is a lovely man, and I look forward to introducing him to our Impact Austin family.

If you never ask, you'll never know. What are you waiting for? Go ask!

*   *   *

In early 2008, the board began the conversation about Impact Austin's future and what my role might be going forward. We wanted to focus on what was best for Impact Austin and philosophically, I understood. Though, it took my heart a lot longer to embrace the change. We formed the Transition Committee which included multiple stakeholders and excluded me with my blessing. I was not prepared for all of the emotions I experienced when the decision about Impact Austin's future was out of my hands. I felt anger, loss, grief and mistrust. I tried not to take things personally and rarely succeeded. Language is powerful, and I used words as weapons that made me feel better in the moment. As a result, I became someone I didn't like and lost some relationships because of it. At first, I vehemently justified my behavior to myself. I felt alone, misunderstood and not appreciated.

My deck became my safe haven, and the barn swallow held me accountable. In that quiet space, I felt welcomed and free to fall apart. I could see what was happening, but I couldn't quell the anger, sense of loss and grief that accompanied the talk about my transition.

He started right in, "Rebecca, you knew this time was coming. Why are you so angry and full of sadness? This is what you've wanted all along."

"I know this is what I've wanted. I don't think I admitted to myself how much of me was wrapped up in Impact Austin and its success. I can see what's happening and how badly I'm behaving.

It's so hard to be excluded from talk about the transition, especially because it impacts me directly."

Predictably he responded, "This seems to be more about trusting others to have both your and Impact Austin's best interests in mind. Why don't you give that some thought?" And, then he took flight as if he'd had enough of my pity party.

I had read a lot about founder's syndrome and others had generously shared what they had learned and knew about it. I was determined not to let it darken Impact Austin's doorstep. Well, knowing and doing are two different things. I had made it very difficult for the Transition Committee to do its job by challenging its recommendations and offering alternative ideas they deemed unworkable. To this day, I believe all of us had Impact Austin's best interest in mind; we just had different perspectives. Unfortunately, my emotional attachment hindered my ability to be rational at times. As a result, the Transition Committee disbanded.

In June, 2008, seven of the twelve board members resigned. For some, their terms had ended. A few left early because they had grown tired of the conflicts that arose—mostly caused by me. This was the beginning of a challenging twenty-four month period when we were trying to figure out our future and the path to get us there.

I struggled with letting go. After all, Impact Austin had become my identity, and I loved every minute of participating in its success. In hindsight, I realize that I didn't trust anyone to care for it the way I did. So, giving up any control was scary. Trusting my cape took on a whole new meaning. I had to believe the right outcome would prevail and that my cape would help me land right where I was supposed to be.

We had accomplished our audacious goal of having 500 members by the end of our fifth year, and I wasn't confident we could keep that up without my participation. Some of that was ego-related. Some of it was knowing I would do whatever it took to make our number and didn't expect others to have the same level of devotion. That old IBM quota monster sat on my shoulder and motivated me to meet any goal—in spite of what others thought was reasonable.

We reorganized in July in an effort to separate governance and operational responsibilities. We saw this as our first step in creating a sustainable business model. The board became strictly a governing and policy-making body. Simultaneously, we created an operations structure, encompassing all volunteer functions. In that first year of transition, I led both bodies as we built out the roles and responsibilities of our new structures. I loved being involved in designing our future, and I embraced this arrangement knowing my time leading the organization was coming to a close.

After raising an additional $150,000 from our members, we invested some of that money in technology to streamline processes and make things more efficient. We reserved the rest, knowing we'd have to pay the next operational leader a reasonable salary. In many cases, the members who contributed to this campaign were women who had not been philanthropic before their membership in Impact Austin and credited Impact Austin with making them philanthropists—no matter what their giving level was. They realized they had the power to make a difference, and my heart still smiles when I think about it.

*   *   *

Meeta, one of the board members who did not resign in June or give up the fight, worked closely with me as we navigated this rocky period. I first met her at a recruiting coffee in November, 2005. There were about a dozen women in attendance, and she intrigued me from the minute she walked in the door right before I began to speak. She seemed a bit aloof, with a hint of "friendly."

One of our board members had invited her, and her demeanor suggested she came out of obligation. She stood in the back of the room expressionless as I shared the Impact Austin story and what we had accomplished in our first two years. Because I had given this recruiting pitch dozens of times, I could scan the room while talking, observe the attendees and pick up on subtle clues as to their level of interest. I knew Meeta was listening because she and I made eye contact a couple of times, and I saw her brow furrow.

When I asked if anyone had questions, she surprised me by stepping forward.

"I just happened to glance at the invitation in a stack of mail on my desk on my way out the door and decided to drop in before running errands. I told my husband I was attending to be polite and had no intention of joining. I'm so glad I came because you seem like an authentic group of women trying to make a difference. This is what I need to be doing right now, and I want to join." By saying that in front of the women assembled, she started a chain reaction, and most joined right along with her.

She and I worked closely during my time of transition out of leadership in 2009 and 2010. She endured some of my not so pretty moments and helped me focus on the bigger picture.

She was not afraid to go toe to toe with me and challenged my thinking regularly. My respect for her grew tremendously, and we established a deep level of trust that has endured. As always, when I surround myself with people smarter than I am and can lower my defenses, that's when I experience the most personal growth.

*   *   *

Growing up, I was a pleaser. When I did what grown-ups expected, I got rewarded and that equaled love to me. My parents ran a very controlled, mannerly household with "yes ma'am" and "yes sir" probably being the first words I learned. They insisted on having polite and well-mannered children, especially out in public.

At the age of seven, I remember eating at Howard Johnson's and one couple coming up to my parents to compliment them on their well-behaved children. At the time, we were eight, seven, four and two. We were trained not to look around at others because it was considered nosy and impolite. We kept our hands folded on the restaurant table and looked straight ahead. If we weren't well-behaved, the consequences were harsh. Needless to say, I learned at an early age that compliance was the least painful path.

And, in the process, I learned that my parents and others liked to be around me because I was good and aimed to please. There was a pay-off in that for me. Because one's parents are normally the first leaders in a kid's life, it never occurred to me that there were other ways to parent and lead. I had lived my parents' model for so long, and it's what I knew.

So, imagine being in a leadership position with my family and Impact Austin, having grown up in an environment where effective leadership to me meant enforcing ironclad rules and expecting strict compliance. That was my initial approach—a bit softened from my childhood days, but when things got "messy" or I didn't know how to handle a certain board member or one of my kids, I'd resort to my controlling persona. I knew how to operate in that arena even though it was less than effective.

My rise to PTA President came about because I was reliable and had the ability to take on a project and get it done on time without errors. I had a strong sense of right versus wrong, was honest and worked hard. These were mistakenly seen as good leadership attributes. I was president for two years, and many of the board members liked my attention to detail and my on-time mentality— especially when it came to starting and ending meetings on time. But, I can't say I made a huge contribution to advancing the PTA leadership model. In fact, I was oblivious to that aspect of my position. I came; I got the work done; I exited. Not much to lean on when building Impact Austin

During my eight years at the helm of Impact Austin, Phil helped me navigate tricky volunteer situations to get the right outcomes. He gave me the words to use and let me practice on him. He never imposed his ideas, but he graciously responded when I asked for help. Most importantly, he taught me to do the right thing even when it was unpopular, uncelebrated and probably even unnoticed.

His advice and support helped me survive the lonely moments like enduring difficult member interactions; burning the midnight oil when a volunteer dropped the ball right before an important deadline and juggling multiple tasks while trying not to let anything slip through the cracks. Most members had no idea how many times I had to step in and help at the last minute. It was all part of what I signed up for, and it didn't bother me until someone confronted me when they didn't know all of the facts.

A member, who played a significant role, called me out of the blue one day and chided me for my ineptness. Her negative tone called me to attention, and my heart started racing.

"Rebecca, you cannot expect me to work with this calendar the way you've designed it."

She explained her myriad reasons for such displeasure, and I listened in silence while taking deep breaths just to stay minimally calm. Conflicts with members were rare, and I wasn't prepared for this.

When she took a breath, I composed myself and replied, "You make some great points, and I appreciate your feedback. Please understand that I'm balancing the needs of everyone who uses the calendar."

She continued to speak with strong words about her frustration, and it started wearing me down. Finally I interrupted, "I am really clear about your concerns, and we need to end this conversation before one of us says something we regret."

When my adrenaline rush subsided, tears formed. I felt disrespected and lonely. As my sadness escalated, I absentmindedly opened a desk drawer only to discover a small bag of cards and kind notes that members had sent me over time. My spirits slowly lifted as I began to read them. From that moment forward, I called it the "Me" bag and still read a few cards from it when times get tough. I believe every leader needs a "Me" bag. It's a lifeline. I'm serious.

Several years later, that disgruntled volunteer sent me a note saying how much she appreciated my leadership and apologized for being unnecessarily hard on me at times. Of course, that note is in my "Me" bag.

*   *   *

Starting in July, 2009, I no longer had a seat on the board. I had reached my six-year limit, though I continued to lead operations as the unpaid CEO. The board was now my boss, and it took me a while to accept and appreciate that relationship. No one was asking my opinion about governance issues anymore. I reported monthly to the board and was judged based on performance metrics they had set. Can't say it was easy or fun for me or them. Impact Austin had a unique value proposition relative to other funders. Our inclusive grassroots approach to philanthropy challenged the norms. There wasn't another entity that could fill the hole left if we were plucked out of the community, and that fueled my passion. Not everyone on the board shared that same level of passion, causing tension which diverted us from focusing on our mission for a while.

Not surprisingly, I headed to my deck one evening to have a conversation with my barn swallow. This time, I was sipping a glass of wine to settle my nerves. "I know there isn't anyone who will ever have the same passion for Impact Austin that I do as the founder. But, I have a hard time accepting anything less. Mostly, because I know we can achieve the goals we've set and keep our high standards."

The swallow's reply got my attention. "Great leaders exhibit personal humility and professional will, and both are in short supply with you right now. Maybe you should reflect on that a bit."

"I am so tired of all the lessons I'm supposed to be learning. I don't want to give up because I'm not a quitter, but I do need to make room for new leaders to appear. I'll think about what you said and examine my heart. It's hurting, too."

Seeing the beauty in the 'mess'

I've never met Terry Hershey. Probably never will. A friend introduced me to him several years ago by forwarding one of his gems. He writes blogs. Really good ones. They challenge my thinking and call me to attention even when I try to resist. Sometimes I laugh out loud; sometimes I reach for a Kleenex. He normally hits a nerve, and I'm positive he feels really good about that! His words seem to jump off the computer screen, bore right through my chest and nestle in my heart.

Recently Terry wrote, "If beauty resides in the mess…it means giving up our need for perfection. It means finding Grace in broken things. It means accepting the blotches and blunders as a part of the whole of our life. It means taking ourselves a lot less seriously. It means not dismissing or diminishing the imperfections, but working them in, creating the exquisite beauty that is our life."

Again, I'm reminded of my Impact Austin journey. So many unknowns lie ahead, but beauty resides in the "mess." This is not a journey for one, but a caravan for many that will reveal horizons unknown and promises our hearts cannot yet imagine. Come along, if you will and keep Terry in mind if you need some inspiration along the way.

7

LETTING GO & PAYING FORWARD

"Strength doesn't come from what you can do.
It comes from overcoming the things you once thought you couldn't."

—Rikki Rogers

I had always promised myself when the joy of leading Impact Austin outweighed the pain, it was time for me to step aside and let others take the reins. I thrive in an environment awash in unknowns, where taking a leap of faith is required. It was fun to build Impact Austin from the ground up—seeing challenges as opportunities for more creativity—not knowing what to expect from one day to the next.

After having accomplished our goal of reaching the 500-member threshold, I took a big deep breath and wondered what was next. We didn't need to grow just for the sake of growing. It was hard enough to steward 500 members well. I decided that we needed to string together another two successful recruiting seasons so that we could sustain that level and continue to give grants in each of our five focus areas. Once that was accomplished, I would step aside.

Claire: my grown-up little girl

Moving Claire into her dorm at college this week has been tough on my emotions. Even though she's a junior, and I've done this with her two times before, I know why this has been the hardest. She could have done it totally without me. So organized, so mature, so capable. She figures out answers to questions before she has to ask, and she's even helping me solve problems that should be my own to solve. Sometimes, I'm not sure who the parent is. What I am sure of is that she loves me and understands my need to be involved in this part of her life, especially if it makes letting go just a teensy bit easier for me, her mom. She is going to be a great mom someday, and I know that for sure because she parents me so well! She will always be a part of me, and me of her—just in a different way. For now, I will draw on this experience as a metaphor for letting go of some responsibilities with Impact Austin. The love affair continues. It's just maturing.

In September, 2010, I informed the board of my desire to retire as of December 31. I agreed to work behind the scenes during the leadership transition in whatever capacity they saw fit. Impact Austin hired an interim executive director, who led operations and helped us write a job description for a permanent leader. We hired our first Executive Director in June, 2011, and the board learned a lot during her two-year tenure. It wasn't easy to follow a founder who had a very public role in the organization. Leading a volunteer-powered organization requires excellent people skills and a certain amount of finesse that only comes with experience.

Impact Austin subsequently hired the previous interim executive director as its full-time leader, and that arrangement worked for several years. With each hire, the board got more clear about the needs of the business and the skills necessary to lead Impact Austin successfully into the future.

Let go and move forward!

Wednesday evening was difficult. I officially handed off my favorite duty as the lead Impact Austin coffee speaker to other energetic members who have a passion for our mission; members who have their own compelling Impact Austin stories to share. I knew, without a doubt, it was the right thing to do for Impact Austin. For me personally, it's been a struggle. I keep asking myself, "Why am I giving up the single, most fun aspect of my job—the part that gives me the greatest joy?" I love evangelizing when I believe in a cause, and I believe in Impact Austin!

As I was preparing remarks for a talk I gave on Thursday, it hit me like a ton of bricks. My opportunity to evangelize had not ended at all. Seeds of Strength (SOS) is a collective giving organization in Georgetown, TX, that has modeled itself after Impact Austin and others like us. The gathering included its members and women they had invited to learn more about the organization. Ninety women—half of whom were prospective members. A gold mine of opportunity for them and me! They had asked me to share whatever I thought would resonate with the audience to get them to join SOS. I shared my personal Impact Austin story, just as I always have. The message didn't change—just the stage. I am not giving up what I love to do. I am expanding my horizons; evangelizing from different pulpits, and it feels right.

*   *   *

I credit Lisa with helping me "let go" of Impact Austin. We had an awkward introduction in February, 2007, when we both spoke on the same panel at a women's conference in Austin. As we approached the dais to take our seats, I introduced myself.

"Hi, Lisa. I'm Rebecca Powers with Impact Austin, and I'm thrilled that your organization, College Forward, has applied for a grant. We love learning about non-profits doing great things in Central Texas."

She dismissively replied, "I'm not aware that we applied. Our grant writer handles all of that." I do remember thinking it was odd that the Executive Director didn't know about the $100,000 grant opportunity they were applying for!

The panel discussion began with each of us introducing ourselves, and I learned that she founded College Forward in 2003 as a result of reading a magazine article in a hotel room after dropping her son off for his freshman year at college. While I read *People* on an airplane instead of a hotel room, our experiences mirrored each other. It was uncanny. When the panel discussion ended, we were deluged with attendees who wanted to speak to us; so, we had no further conversation—until College Forward received an Impact Austin grant that June. I asked her to go to lunch to get to know her a bit and to thank her for what she was doing in the community for high school students who were the first in their families to go to college.

During that lunch she came clean. "Rebecca, when we met at that conference, I totally knew College Forward had applied for the Impact Austin grant because I wrote the damn thing! You intimidated me by your outgoing style, and I didn't want to say anything that would lessen our chances of staying in the running. Now, I want to be a member of this organization and hang with you neat ladies. Here's my membership check."

We still laugh about the charade she pulled when we first met, and I'm not sure who laughs louder. Over time, she and I became confidantes, and I turned to her when I wanted to check my ego or talk about leadership challenges. She never turned me down and always had something pithy to say. When it was time for me to step down from my leadership role with Impact Austin, I wrestled with the fact that my head knew it was time to go, but my heart wasn't following as quickly. I found myself worrying about every little aspect of the organization and if the interim executive director we had hired would remember all that I told her or if she'd even read the binders of information I painstakingly put together. More than once, Lisa talked about two trapezes, saying I had to let go of one before I could grab the other. I'd have to fully let go of Impact Austin before I could embrace what was next. Her analogy helped me through that really difficult time.

We both turned sixty the same year and decided to commemorate that milestone by enjoying an "Excellent Adventure" each month. In August, we drove a U-Haul truck with all of Claire's belongings from Austin to San Diego in less than thirty hours. While that was a blast with lots of laughs and plenty of windshield time, our trip to Eagle, CO, in July provided much more entertainment. We learned to fly fish, did some white water rafting and attended our first rodeo. We are not particularly athletic women, so it shocked friends when Lisa posted pictures of us on Facebook in very treacherous rapids. She had found a picture online where you couldn't make out the people in the raft. The comments were funny, and her replies were funnier. To her credit, she never admitted it was a stock photo. She also posted a picture of someone in a turquoise shirt perched on a bucking bronco. It's my favorite color, and she said I was riding that untamed beast. No one believed her, but it didn't matter. We were totally entertained and enjoyed spoofing our friends. We now try to go on one excellent adventure each year—just to keep the tradition alive. Making memories with someone who has been through the fire with me, who knows me intimately and who continually challenges me to reach for the next trapeze is a friend I want for life. In fact she recently moved back to West Texas and started a collective giving group in Midland. I couldn't ask for a better example of Impact Austin's influence in women's lives as they find their power in giving back.

The Rainbow

Peter spoke to me through a new song yesterday. I was in my car lamenting my difficult last couple of weeks....

After an appointment ended early, I returned to my car with some bonus free time to enjoy. I decided to just sit in the driver's seat and throw myself a pretty decent impromptu pity party. No balloons. No streamers. No clowns. Just my determination to sit there and really feel my despair. Out of habit, I turned on the radio, and that's when the pity party ended. The song that started at the **exact** *moment I turned on the music was "Somewhere over the Rainbow" by Israel "IZ" Kamakawiwo'ole. Tears streamed down my face as I stared at the sunshine, rolled down my windows and sang at the top of my voice. (Thank goodness I was parked in a remote location away from other humans.) In 3 minutes and 47 seconds, my mood changed. Peter was perched atop my left shoulder reminding me that all's well. I had been looking for the rainbow, and it showed up in spades. I couldn't have scripted this better.*

The pain of the last two weeks has not disappeared completely, but I am reminded of friends and family who care about me. Time is the great healer, and I am leaning on that wise saying heavily while I look for more rainbows. Peter, you amaze me, and I love you!

PS: I know the song is 3:47 long because I listened to it on You-Tube when I got home. I won't say how many times.

*　　　*　　　*

In early 2017, the board accepted the resignation of its second Executive Director and decided to reflect a bit before making another permanent hire. A board member raised her hand and generously offered to act as the interim ED until Impact Austin was ready to hire someone permanently. That gave the board some breathing room, and they used it wisely.

Lauren had just returned to Impact Austin as a member and soon joined the board right when some critical decisions were being made. Lauren was a strategic thinker and had led the Marketing Committee previously. Her leadership in past years had paid dividends, and they wanted her back in a decision-making role on the board. Thankfully, she agreed.

I met Lauren in 2007, a newlywed in her twenties, over lunch after being introduced by a mutual friend. I was excited to share the Impact Austin story with her and could tell she was interested in joining because her body leaned forward as she asked great questions. She said if she joined, she wanted to sit on a grant review committee and possibly do something else after that. However, the $1000 investment was going to be a stretch. I asked if she could afford a $500 investment, and she thought that was doable. I offered to personally match her $500 the first year. She agreed that if she had a good experience and wanted to continue her membership the following year that she would invest a full $1000 on her own. In hindsight, it's one of the best investments I ever made on behalf of Impact Austin.

When Lauren returned to Impact Austin, I had been on the sidelines for seven years and had a general sense of how things were going, but I didn't know details. Our membership attainment each year had been on a slow decline, and Lauren knew we could do better. She asked me to re-engage and help Impact Austin return to our 500-member status. I convinced Phylis to partner with me just like we did in the early years. We knew it would take two years to get us back to 500 members, and we didn't waste a minute. We accomplished our goal in that two years and immediately retired from that role for the final time.

As a board member, Lauren brought structure and process. She realized there were some key skills missing that would make the board more effective, and she knew some members with those skills who might be interested in serving in that capacity. After a few months, the board chair resigned due to family health issues, and Lauren took on that role. Soon, there were new faces and fresh ideas percolating regarding Impact Austin's future and how to get there. The board invited me to join because there was a lack of institutional knowledge, and I was thrilled to accept. I served two years and enjoyed getting back into a rhythm that I had missed for several years.

One of the new board's first priorities was hiring an executive director. This time, Impact Austin hired a search firm that specialized in sourcing nonprofit leaders. The fee for their search was steep, based on our budget. Though, the board agreed that we had to get this hire right, and we didn't have the bandwidth or expertise to conduct a successful search on our own.

Lauren asked me to chair the search committee and work closely with the search firm. I accepted and did cartwheels in my office, but I didn't tell anyone! Our committee included another board member, a past board member and three stakeholders from the community, which provided many different perspectives relative to the candidates. We chose two finalists who made a presentation to the board and then answered some questions. It was a unanimous decision to hire Christina. She is smart, values relationships and cares genuinely for the underserved. She's an unapologetic feminist with charisma and class.

During the search process and before we met any of the candidates, Christina asked the search firm if she could meet the founder to learn more about Impact Austin's history. At first, I was reluctant because I didn't want it to seem like one candidate got special treatment over another. In the end, I decided to have coffee with her since she took the initiative to ask. Though, I did choose a coffee spot that was not in my normal orbit just to keep it on the down low. Sneaky, I know. I was already seated and facing the front door when a young woman wearing a bright yellow top entered. She gave off a very positive and friendly vibe before she reached the table. I knew it had to be Christina.

She started, "You must be Rebecca, and I'm so pleased to meet you. Thank you for giving me the opportunity to get to know you and your motivation for starting such an incredible organization."

There was something so genuine about her demeanor, and I was caught off-guard. The conversation flowed as if we were old friends catching up, and I appreciated her desire to get to know me, focusing less attention on the ins and outs of Impact Austin.

After I answered her initial questions, she continued, "I believe this job was written just for me and here are the reasons...."

It was a gentle, thoughtful conversation that made me feel like she wanted to care for and grow the organization I had birthed. Right before we parted ways, she inquired, "Will you tell me more about your brother, Peter?" Of course I obliged, and she still reminds me of what I told her about him on occasion. It's pretty cool.

I never told the search committee that she and I had that conversation. I didn't want it to skew anyone's thinking before I learned what they thought of her after her first interview. I also knew they would see her heart for service and her understanding of our mission all on their own.

When I retired from the board this time, my head **and** my heart left full of joy and with the confidence that Impact Austin was in good hands under Lauren's board leadership and with Christina as our Executive Director. Lauren was the right person at the right time to set us up for success, and I will always think of her as the catalyst for that positive change. Some of us lovingly still refer to her as our Impact Austin unicorn—a rare find, indeed! During her tenure, we recovered from our setbacks and have become even stronger than before. She has now retired from the board, but not before ensuring her successor would continue the positive forward momentum she initiated.

What started back in 2003 as an experiment in a petri dish called Austin, TX, is now an established funding source that Central Texas counts on each year. An executive director of one of our grant recipients said to me, "I don't know what Kool-Aid you are feeding your members, but it must be one of a kind because you are a new breed of philanthropists, and it's refreshing." That confirmed for me that our grand experiment was working.

The view from 30,000 feet

I am 30,000 feet above the earth right now. Same place I was seven years ago when the seed of Impact Austin was planted. So much has changed, and none of it is lost on me.

Then: *I was returning to Austin in the dark of night, alone with my fears, anger and sadness. I couldn't see anything out the window. I had no idea what the future held. I wasn't certain at all what to do with the emotions I was feeling and dreaded knowing that I'd have to face the reality of my brother Peter and his certain death soon, which occurred three weeks later. I decided to lean on the People article I had just read and the hope it gave me—smiling involuntarily as I learned about the women who were so excited to give and the dental clinic that was so excited to receive.*

Now: I am flying midday with the sun shining brightly. The plane is dancing between puffy cumulus clouds, and my heart is happy. I can see for miles out the window. No feelings of fear, anger or sadness. At times, I know I see Peter, dancing in the arms of the angels as they prance from cloud to cloud. Peter comes back to me many times through songs I hear randomly on my iPod. Sometimes, he will sit on my shoulder and give me words of wisdom and the courage to keep going. It usually happens when I'm struggling with a business decision or fretting over a family dilemma. He calms my nerves and helps me see more clearly. I smile to myself and giggle about his ability to still 'brother' me.

Next: The next chapter of my life is almost here, and I can't wait! The pages are still blank, but Peter will guide me as I go. Sometimes he does it with humor. Sometimes he acts like a know-it-all. I listen nonetheless. It feels good to know he has his eye on me.

I love you, Peter.

*   *   *

I didn't go searching for this journey. It found me and fundamentally changed my heart. With childlike wonder, I marvel at the gifts I've received and lovingly share what I've learned with anyone who asks. I consider it a privilege and believe it's my calling to inspire women across the country to take a leap of faith like I did, walking beside them as they begin to believe they can do what we did in Austin. I take no credit for their success. I just want to be the wind beneath their wings like God has been for me. And, it doesn't hurt to trust your cape in the process.

Paying my success forward has taken me all across the country, and a few of those noteworthy experiences are shared below.

*   *   *

The Associate Director of the Parents Campaign at The George Washington University, where Claire attended college, contacted me via email. He was making a swing through Central Texas and wanted to introduce himself, inquire about our experience as parents of a student there and share an update about the school. All of it as a prelude to asking for a contribution—at least to my way of thinking. I decided to give him the courtesy of one meeting because I knew the drudgery of making cold calls, which I had done as an IBM sales rep.

Our conversation was memorable for two reasons. First, he didn't ask me for money. Second, he had prepared well. He knew about Impact Austin and wanted to know more. He also took notes and showed genuine interest when I shared some thoughts about Claire's experience at GW. When our meeting ended, he asked if he could follow up with me the next time he was in Texas. It was easy to say "yes".

Simultaneously, GW was planning a Women and Philanthropy Forum, and he recommended me as a speaker. The Impact Austin story intrigued him, and he thought it would inspire any woman who attended the Forum, regardless of her means. The fact that I was also the parent of a current student made me an attractive candidate.

While other speakers had family foundations and more traditional philanthropic experiences, the grassroots nature of Impact Austin—how we started and what we had learned about philanthropy as a result—resonated with many of the Forum attendees. That speaking experience affirmed two things: agreeing to that first visit with Ted was a really smart decision, and the Impact Austin story continues to inspire women to find their power in giving back.

A year later, a woman who had attended the Forum asked me to speak at an upcoming CASE (Council for Advancement and Support of Education) conference to be held in Pittsburgh, PA. I eagerly accepted the invitation and realized that I still got to inspire audiences with the Impact Austin story. It was just from a different stage. First GW, next the CASE Conference. And then....

Shepherd University Foundation in Shepherdstown, WV, came calling. Some of their staff attended my breakout session at the CASE conference and liked what they heard. The Executive Vice President of the Foundation invited me to share the Impact Austin story with their Women for Shepherd donors.

Arriving on campus, I knew where to go because I found my headshot staring back at me from the marquis in front of the building where I would speak. Oh, Lord! Imposter syndrome rattled my nerves. "If they only knew who I was—I don't deserve this treatment." Shaking off my doubt, I took a deep breath, straightened my jacket and pretended I was going to an Impact Austin recruiting coffee, which I had done with ease so many times before. The women asked great questions and showed interest in creating a giving circle there. While I was happy to answer questions and encourage them to pursue their idea, I didn't expect to develop a close relationship with them going forward. I was wrong.

Four women spearheaded the formation of the WISH (Women Investing in Shepherd) giving circle, and I joined them on a series of conference calls to share best practices as they strategized about recruiting and grantmaking. I encouraged them to think big and set a target of one hundred members by year end. Finding that many women to invest seemed to them like a really steep mountain to climb, but they accepted the challenge. They counted 105 women as members their first year and celebrated the powerful statement it made in their small community. I attended their first award ceremony and celebrated with them. As a result, I joined WISH that day and have been a member ever since. It gives me a chance to stay in touch and watch them grow.

*   *   *

A woman from California attended our fifth Annual Meeting, the first time we awarded five $100,000 grants. It was a big deal, and the excitement was palpable. A member snuck her in (we didn't allow guests back then), and by the end of the evening she decided to start a like organization in Laguna Beach, where she lived. Phil had recently won a local golf tournament that qualified him for one near Laguna Beach, and I planned to join him. Talk about a wonderful coincidence, though I prefer to think of it as a God wink. We agreed to meet and talk in even more detail. A year later, Impact Giving held its first member meeting, and I attended to show support and cheer them on.

On a subsequent visit, I sat next to a woman on my flight who asked what I did for a living. I explained the collective giving concept and my reason for visiting California that day. She lived in Orange County and decided to join Impact Giving in midair, already thinking of two women she would ask to join as well. It reminded me to never stop evangelizing. Inviting women to find their power in giving back can happen anywhere.

*   *   *

In 2010, an Impact Austin member connected me with a relatively informal giving circle in Boston. The leaders were reimagining their giving model and wanted to learn more about us and our structure. Over the course of several months, we conversed by phone which culminated in a trip to Boston to participate in a roundtable discussion with their members. What happened next can only be described as serendipity or as another God wink.

A year later, one of the Boston leaders met Allison, who was born and raised in Austin, on a two-week trek in Peru and shared a bit about her connection to me and Impact Austin. Allison contacted me upon her return to say she wanted to join Impact Austin and explained her connection to the Boston woman.

Ironically, Allison lived in Chicago most of the year and visited her parents occasionally in Austin. She wanted to participate in our grant review process and flew back to Austin for each of the four committee meetings over the course of five months, taking full advantage of Southwest Airlines' promotional $29 fares in the process. She subsequently shared her experience with trusted friends back in Chicago, and they formed Impact Grants Chicago, which is going gangbusters.

The power of connection cannot be understated. Austin to Boston to Machu Picchu and back to Austin, then Chicago. The willingness to share and inspire makes us all better. My life has been enhanced immeasurably by my involvement in collective giving. The last blog I ever wrote still brings tears to my eyes when I read it. I love you, Impact Austin!

With tears flowing for all
the right reasons

Dear Impact Austin,

My, how you've grown up...!

*I remember naming you before you were born. Standing in my bathrobe at the kitchen counter, looking into the back yard and dreaming about a future with you that would make life **very** interesting. You were born on May 28, 2003, and I could not have been prouder! That birth certificate, the Articles of Incorporation, has been shown to many and copied for anyone who needed proof that you exist. Your birth family, the founding board members, cooed at your arrival, and then they got busy! The bylaws, marketing brochures, grant application and review processes, member recruitment—were all created before you took your first few steps. You had **many** mothers, and you were a good baby.*

Toddlerhood was a different story. You weren't always compliant, and you could be stubborn. I had to learn how to handle you, and I was often clumsy. But children are resilient, and you continued to love me. You taught me patience and forgiveness along the way, and I appreciate that about you.

I realize now that I have taught you all I can. It's time for me to let you spread your wings and grow into the beautiful butterfly I have imagined all along. You have the support of the entire family, old and young. I will always be near. I will always care. You can count on me to listen when you get frustrated and celebrate with you when you accomplish great things. Your spirit is contagious, and your followers will grow in number. May you never take anyone for granted and may you always be warm and welcoming...the way you've been since the day you were born.

I love you now and forever—no matter what.

Mom

CONCLUSION

"...becoming isn't about arriving somewhere...
the journey doesn't end."

—Michelle Obama

One of my close childhood friends, Shelley, who still lives in Central Illinois, knew about Impact Austin ever since our early days. She always wanted updates and shared in my joy as we built and grew the organization. In 2018, Phil and I attended her daughter's wedding in the Douro River Valley in Portugal and stayed at an inn nestled in a vineyard. It was a magical setting; the intimate outdoor wedding was beautiful with grapes growing all around us. I still have close-up pictures on my phone of the luscious grapevines I passed as I walked through those vineyards each morning. We arrived a couple of days early and had a lovely dinner that first evening with the bride's parents and a few others.

As we were all getting acquainted, the topic of Impact Austin came up and someone at the table wanted to know more. I gushed about how it had changed me and our members in such a powerful way. I also shared the joy I experienced when working with women in other cities as they created their own collective giving organizations. After eating some delicious food and enjoying extraordinary port produced at that vineyard, we retired to our rooms.

The next morning, we all took a two-hour cruise on the Douro River. The scenery was breathtaking, and it never got old. Phil and I sat in amazement appreciating the fact that we got to experience this with others who felt the same sense of wonder. Shelley's sister-in-law, Laurie, approached me about an hour into the cruise and wanted to know even more about Impact Austin than she had learned at dinner the night before.

She pulled up a chair next to where I was sitting and faced me directly. I could tell this was not going to be a casual conversation just to pass the time. She had already started thinking about creating a giving circle when she got back home. She asked insightful questions and wanted to know all of the challenges we faced when we started. I told her that while the concept was simple and easy to understand, the successful implementation of the model required more work than one might imagine. We talked about specifics, and I encouraged her to gather a group of women who might be interested in investing and helping her build out the organization.

She responded instantly, "I'm only going to do this if Shelley will do it with me." I knew they'd make a great team, though I didn't know what Shelley's appetite would be for jumping in with both feet. The conversation ended, and we didn't speak about it again on that trip.

Once back home, Shelley agreed to jump in though she was nervous about the time commitment and how difficult it might be to get women to join. Caterpillar had just moved its world headquarters from Peoria to Chicago, which created lots of economic uncertainty. Would women be willing to invest $1000 in their initiative? Shelley and Laurie invited several women for dinner to explore the idea. I attended and shared the Impact Austin story, answering questions and encouraging the women to dream big. It was magical to see them take hold of an idea, brainstorm a bit and decide to use their talents and intellect to turn the dream into reality.

At that dinner, I used the assumptive approach by stating, "**When** you start recruiting members, you might want to have a target. We set a goal of 124 members our first year because the organization we learned about in the *People* article had 123 founding members. We overachieved and welcomed 126 women that first year."

One of the dinner guests immediately piped up, "I guess our goal is at least 127!" They were off and running!

Early on, I connected these women with Allison, the Impact Austin member that co-founded Impact Grants Chicago. Allison invited the Peoria team to visit so they could see how another established collective giving organization operated. Allison and her Chicago team welcomed them warmly, sharing their set-up in great detail.

Allison also hosted a gathering at her home in Austin for the Central Illinois women to meet the Impact Austin founding board members and ask even more questions when they were in town for Impact Austin's 2019 Annual Meeting. They wanted to see how we handled the grant finalist presentations and subsequent voting process and left town the next day with heads full of new information and lots of ideas. They also left with hearts full of gratitude and hope.

Not surprisingly, on June 9, 2020, Impact Central Illinois' 130 members extended their first grant of $130,000 to Children's Home to revitalize its Youth Farm location. It's so inspiring to see the result of women lifting other women up, which makes us all better. The magic continues!

*   *   *

As a grassroots start-up in 2003, the founding board had no idea if our giving model would take hold. We believed in it, but that wasn't enough to ensure its long-term success. We agreed that we had to string at least three successful grantmaking cycles together, which meant our grant recipients had to successfully implement the programs we funded. When we achieved that milestone, we focused on growth and the goal of counting 500 women as members by year five, which we did. Quickly, our efforts turned from growth to sustainability.

While we had talked about the importance of an endowment, we didn't want to start one until we believed in our sustainability. Asking women to invest in our long-term success seemed premature until we knew we could keep the business funded and running well year over year.

In April, 2016, one of our board members seeded the endowment with $10,000. Sara had won a professional award and gifted it to Impact Austin. She and I first met at our Rotary Club ten years earlier, and I learned a lot about leadership from her example. Like Impact Austin, Rotary is volunteer-powered, and she had presided over a chapter in California as its President before moving to Austin and eventually becoming President of our club. She and I served on a committee together, which is when I learned about the importance of an endowment and its ability to provide permanence for an organization. She saw the endowment as a way to introduce our members to another way to give back that would ensure Impact Austin's legacy.

As a result, we now have one that continues to grow steadily as our members and others make investments. In fact, a portion of the proceeds from the sale of this book will continue to feed our endowment and also provide operating funds for other women's organizations across the country.

*   *   *

While founding Impact Austin had not been a lifelong dream of mine, it was clearly my calling and where I found my purpose. It was born of a need to fill the hole in my heart, and I also believe it helped fill the hole in my parents' hearts. My father, a closet poet, wrote these words in 2011, a year before his death, to celebrate this journey.

For Pete's Sake

A deep love never dies.
Never disappears,
But gathers up with strong desire
To live beyond the tears.

Returning home with heavy heart
Her love and grief collided,
Gave birth to Impact Austin –
A new life, God provided.

Women by the hundreds
Opened up their hearts and purses,
As love of others came alive
To deal with life's reverses.

Rebecca must be humbled
To've had this stellar task,
God chose someone who rose — and said
"It's not too much to ask."

With pride, joy and love,
Fithie

Jeremiah 29:11 "For I know the plans I have for you," declares the LORD, "plans to prosper you and not to harm you, plans to give you hope and a future."

I still talk to the barn swallow on my deck when life presents challenges. I didn't feel the need to name him until recently. Now, I call him Noel, which is Peter's middle name. Peter sits on my left shoulder. Noel sits on the deck railing. They work together to help me navigate tricky times. They're an impressive duo, and I'm one lucky gal to have both of them on my team.

About that cape…we normally think of a cape as something worn on the outside, but what I've learned is it's really the fabric on the inside that gives us our power—like grit, spunk, moxie—whatever you want to call it. It's that fighting spirit inside us that whispers "keep going" even when we think we can't. What's your cape made of?

REBECCA POWERS
AUTHOR, SPEAKER, SOCIAL ENTREPRENEUR

Over the past 18 years, Rebecca has inspired thousands of women to connect their capacity to give with the confidence to do it well. Dozens of collective giving organizations have sought out her expertise and mentorship based on a giving model she adopted and made her own. Rebecca is a well-recognized speaker who captivates audiences with storytelling about her personal experiences that create real impact to thrive. She will make you laugh; she will make you cry; she will inspire you to believe in yourself.

For more detailed information on hiring Rebecca for your next event, please contact us at: trustyourcapebook@gmail.com